Advance Praise for MAGAcademy

"Higdon weaves together personal experiences and decades of scholarship into a narrative that is sharp, brave, and, at times, thrilling. He draws on a wide-array of sources, from philosophical treatises to sociological studies to TikTok videos, revealing an omnivorous intellectual appetite that strengthens his argumentation. The assessment of the state of Higher Ed he offers might seem bleak to some, but for those of us working in higher ed right now, particularly as contingent faculty, it will undoubtedly resonate and, one hopes, stir us all to collective action."

> — **Caroline Luce**, Ph.D., Project Director and Lecturer, University of California, Los Angeles, Institute for Research on Labor and Employment

"Higher education is in crisis, but not exactly for the reasons that seem to garner the most attention in our fickle, mediated world. A veteran "road" scholar, Higdon writes accurately and scathingly about the neoliberal professional managerial class of opportunists, careerists, and virtue signalers who executed a slow motion controlled demolition of the academy from the inside. I've lived it and seen it up close for 25 years and this book simply nails it, sometimes hilariously (because no one should have to cry all the time). Corporate grifters have no place in higher ed. Masterfully framed with a foreword by critical scholar Henry Giroux, and bookended with real and achievable proposals to rebuild education in the public interest, Higdon's *MAGAcademy* is a must read for anyone concerned with the future of education and critical scholarship not to mention democracy itself."

> — **Mickey Huff**, Distinguished Director, Park Center for Independent Media; Professor of Journalism, Roy H. Park School of Communications, Ithaca College; Executive Director, Project Censored; and President, Media Freedom Foundation

"Once again, Higdon has peeled back the curtain of an institution with which we may feel a certain familiarity, especially for those of us on the inside, and written an incisive criticism that forces us to look more closely at our day-to-day professional and personal lived experiences. Through Higdon's lens, it becomes clear that seemingly small choices of the past have huge impacts on today, many of them negative. Never one to dwell in pessimism, he also provides readers with ways to push back and reverse the harmful course of those decisions. Blending critical history, pedagogy, analysis, and autoethnography, Higdon paints a picture of higher education that we must look at closely, both to understand ourselves better and to make productive and holistic, humane change."

> — **Allison Butler**, PhD, Senior Lecturer & Associate Chair, and Director Media Literacy Certificate Program in the Department of Communication University of Massachusetts, Amherst

"Anyone who works in a university in the United States today knows that higher education is in crisis. In *MAGAcademy*, Nolan Higdon offers a cogent explanation of how we got here, what the consequences are, and what we might do about it. Through the lens of his own experience as non-tenured faculty, Higdon moves beyond culture wars and moral panics to explain the neoliberal university's institutional failings. The adjunctification of faculty and the explosion of non-sensical administrative positions have devalued education, making our universities prime targets for right-wing authoritarian control. With often humorous anecdotes, clear historical context, and jargon-free analysis, *MAGAcademy* paints a portrait of our academic institutions that will be painfully recognizable to those on the inside and illuminating to those on the outside. Offering strong proposals for how to remake higher education in a post-neoliberal era, Higdon's book should be required reading for professors, students, and anyone who cares about building a democratic future."

> — **Brian Dolber**, Associate Professor of Communication and Media Studies, California State University, San Marcos

"With clarity and elegance Nolan Higdon explains how an uneducated authoritarian President came to wield such great power over our institutions of higher learning. Higdon lays out the market-based pressures, long in the making, that led to Trump's MAGAcademy. Boards of Directors from the moneyed class, corporate consultants preaching the bottom line and eager administrators willing to implement policies hostile to educational principles had already hollowed out American universities. White House demands for ideological fealty in exchange for continued funding was just the last trade off in this decades-long process of compromise. Writing at times from an insider's view he is an active participant at the heart of the struggle, detailing the fight to preserve open debate and free expression, as anti-genocide protests were soon to be shut down on college and university campuses. In the end, Higdon offers ways to rebuild higher education through our collective refusal to accept the logic of the market as inevitable."

> — **Robin Andersen**, Professor Emerita of Media Studies at
> Fordham University,

"While many people focus on the 2nd Trump Administration Higdon effectively illustrates that the neoliberal assault on higher education began decades ago. This has both slowed down the progress of knowledge and commodified education causing students to be unprepared for the job market. The neoliberal assault has led to an overreliance on (often exploited) contingent faculty while many full-time academics prioritize careerism. Higdon does not just offer a critique he offers seven thoughtful proposals to undo the damage. This book is highly recommended for anyone passionate about higher education and may offer a way for conservatives and liberals to find common ground."

> — **Jan-Martijn Meij**, PhD, Associate Professor of Sociology,
> Florida Gulf Coast University

"Dr. Nolan Higdon has brought us a brave and heartfelt critique of the current state of higher education in the U.S. This fiercely honest book is likely to upset many liberals and conservatives alike. By taking on the so-called sacred cows of academia like Student Accommodations and Success Centers, and DEI offices, Higdon exposes that history didn't begin with the election of Donald Trump. His well-researched and articulated arguments detail how decades of neoliberal practices in higher education actually cleared the way and set the agenda for the MAGAfication of academia. Drawing on his own extensive experience in higher education, alongside original survey research, and historical and political economic analysis, Higdon shines a bright light on the failures of most colleges and universities in the U.S., and the ways they have embraced an ever-expanding bureaucratic apparatus, administrative bloat, increasing surveillance and control of both faculty and students, and absurd procedures that must be followed while they distract faculty from the core responsibilities of teaching and scholarship. Dr. Higdon also explores the divide and conquer strategies of neoliberal institutions that pit tenured and tenure track faculty against the precarious non-tenured part-time faculty that now provide the bulk of the instruction in most colleges and universities in the U.S. He illustrates how the modern corporate university that treats students as customers and faculty as customer service representatives is unable to push back against the often-exaggerated criticism coming from the right. And he ends this important and timely book with a blueprint for getting out of the mess that those of us in higher education have largely created for ourselves. Digging down into the key issues affecting modern academia, this is a radical book, in the original sense of the word, and one that doesn't flinch from confronting how the MAGA agenda emerged as a doppelgänger of the neoliberalism manifested by the modern establishment Democratic Party."

— **Bill E Yousman**, Ph.D. Professor of Communication & Media, Sacred Heart University

"*MAGAcademy* is both a history of higher education's corporatization and a deep analysis of the crises facing American universities as Trump seeks to dismantle them. Higdon traces the neoliberal policies and practices that transformed campuses into market-driven institutions, underscoring the complicity of the institutions themselves as he details the damage done. Most importantly, the book does not include a call to merely reject Trumpism in order to restore the status quo. Instead it offers concrete proposals "to reclaim higher education from corporate control and realign it to truly serve the people." Writing with clarity and authority, Higdon blends historical evidence, personal anecdote, and data analysis–into what he calls "memoir and manifesto"–to make *MAGAcademy* both an engaging and urgent read."

> — **Katie Rodger**, President of the University Council-American Federation of Teachers (UC-AFT), University of California, Davis

"Higdon's timely project examines how contemporary higher education has been reshaped by hyper-rational market logic, mismanaged managerial governance, and corporate influence. It explores the sharp growth of administrative power, the casualization of academic labor, and the erosion of academic freedom, situating these developments within longer histories of neoliberal reform. Combining nuanced historical context with sharp institutional analysis, Higdon challenges common assumptions about efficiency, accountability, and "student success," while showing how universities have been reoriented away from public knowledge and democratic inquiry. Rather than nostalgia or partisan critique, it offers a structural explanation of how today's academy functions— and why meaningful reform requires confronting its underlying political economy."

> — **John Corbally**, Ph.D., Professor of History, Diablo Valley College

"In *MAGAcademy,* Nolan Higdon rejects the notion that Trumpism is an external threat to higher education. Offering both "memoir and manifesto," he powerfully reframes the debate and argues that the alignment of fascist politics and academic corporatism is the logical endpoint of systems that neoliberal administrators built from the 1970s to the present. Drawing on his experience as a "freeway flier" teaching across multiple campuses, he offers an insider's perspective on the corporate gutting and the marketization of education that left faculty powerless and students surveilled. Today, 68% of faculty work in precarious adjunct positions, while students struggle with $1.7 trillion in student loan debt. Yet Higdon offers hope: mandate that 90% of instructional hours be taught by tenure-track faculty, reject technological fetishism, rebuild the civic university as a democratic anchor, and fund tuition-free education through wealth and excise taxes. This is essential and urgent reading for reclaiming colleges and universities as democratic public goods."

> — **Nicholas L. Baham III,** Ph.D., Professor of Ethnic Studies at California State University, East Bay

"Media critic and analyst Nolan Higdon, a university professor gives readers a front row seat to what is really happening in America. The book is both a trip through his broad experience and a revealing look inside a world many don't know or recognize. His insight is eye-opening. I found myself saying: "I had no idea." And many will probably think the same thing as they read *"MAGAcademy: How Corporatism Paved the Way for the Hostile Takeover of Higher Ed'.* Critical inquiry seems to be AWOL at a time when many of us don't have the "media literacy" to recognize the moves, in front of and behind the curtain, that are changing institutions like never before. Higdon is the perfect intellectual in the vein of the late Robert McChesney. Both want citizens to open their eyes to the real forces at work, as well as those who fall in line and parrot the official line."

> — **Frank Baker**, Media Literacy Clearing House

Also by Nolan Higdon

Books

Surveillance Education: Navigating the Conspicuous Absence of Privacy in Schools (2025), Co-authored with Mickey Huff.

The Media and Me: A Guide to Critical Media Literacy for Young People (2022), Co-authored with Project Censored.

Let's Agree to Disagree: A Critical Thinking Guide to Communication, Conflict Management, and Critical Media Literacy (2022) , Co-authored with Mickey Huff.

The Podcaster's Dilemma: Decolonizing Podcasters in the Era of Surveillance Capitalism (2021) , Co-authored with Nicholas Baham III.

The Anatomy of Fake News: A Critical News Literacy Education (2020)

United States of Distraction: Media Manipulation in Post-Truth America (And What We Can Do About It) (2019), Co-authored with Mickey Huff.

Digital Media & Podcasts

Gaslight Gazette: A newsletter on Substack (Nolanhigdon.substack.com)

The Disinfo Detox Podcast: Host (YouTube.com/DisinfoDetox)

MAGAcademy, companion podcast, (NolanHigdon.com/MAGAcademy).

First published 2026
by Third Rail Communications
Martinez, CA 94553
© 2026 Nolan Higdon
The right of Nolan Higdon to be identified as the author
of this work has been asserted in accordance with sections
77 and 78 of the Copyright, Designs and Patents Act 1988.

Library of Congress Cataloging-in-Publication Data
A catalog record for this title has been requested
ISBN: 979-8-218-92317-4 (pbk)
ISBN: 979-8-218-92318-1 (ebk)
Cover Design by Adam Armstrong

MAGAcademy

How Corporatism Paved the Way for the Hostile Takeover of Higher Ed

Nolan Higdon

Third Rail Communications

Table of Contents

Higher Education at the Breaking Point

Henry A. Giroux

This is a necessary book, and it arrives at precisely the moment when necessity has become indistinguishable from urgency. *MAGAcademy: How Corporatism Paved the Way for the Hostile Takeover of Higher Education* offers more than an account of institutional decline. It offers a devastating diagnosis of how the slow violence of neoliberalism prepared the ground for an openly authoritarian assault on higher education as a democratic public sphere, however fragile. In doing so, it forces readers to confront a truth long avoided, namely that the current crisis facing colleges and universities did not begin with Trump, nor can it be explained solely by right-wing extremism. It was decades in the making.

For more than forty years, higher education has been hollowed out by market logics that redefined education as a private investment rather than a public good, students as customers rather than citizens, and faculty as managed labor rather than intellectuals entrusted with the work of critical inquiry the mission of educating informed and knowledgeable citizens. What this book makes unmistakably clear is that neoliberal corporatism did not simply weaken universities: it reengineered them. Governance was centralized, bureaucracies proliferated, shared power eroded, and the ethical mission of higher education was displaced by the imperatives of branding, risk management, and profit extraction. In this transformed landscape, authoritarianism did not arrive as an alien force. It arrived as a normalized extension of existing corporate power.

What makes this book especially powerful is its historical depth and intellectual clarity. It shows how decades of corporatism emaciated higher education from within, producing the very institutional logics, managerial technologies, and political vulnerabilities that later made universities uniquely susceptible to Donald Trump's authoritarian demands. Long before Trump issued executive orders or threatened funding, universities had already internalized a language of compliance, risk management, and depoliticized "neutrality" that left them defenseless against overt political coercion. In this sense, *MAGAcademy* does not treat Trumpism as an aberration but as the predictable culmination of neoliberal restructuring and as a precondition for turning higher education into laboratories of far-right indoctrination.

Equally important, this project stands in direct and generative conversation with a body of critical scholarship that has long warned of these dangers. It builds powerfully on analyses of neoliberalism as a cultural and pedagogical force, of authoritarianism as a mode of governance that thrives on institutional hollowing out, and of higher education as a contested democratic public sphere under siege. By extending this work into the concrete terrain of contemporary university governance, labor precarity, surveillance, and repression, the book deepens and advances an intellectual tradition committed not only to critique, but to democratic possibility.

The brilliance of this book lies in its refusal to separate structure from lived experience. Drawing on frontline encounters with administrators, students, faculty, and unions, the author reveals how bureaucratic rationality functions as a pedagogy in its own right, one that teaches compliance, fear, and political resignation. The language of "best practices," "student success," "safety," and "process" becomes a weapon precisely because it masquerades as neutrality. Knowledge is instrumentalized, critical thinking is tamed, critical ideas are banished, and the classroom is transformed into a dead zone of the imagination. Under the banner of care, dissent is criminalized. Under the guise of inclusion, academic freedom is narrowed. Under the promise of efficiency, education is emptied of its democratic content.

What *MAGAcademy* shows with remarkable clarity is how this erosion of democratic purpose left institutions defenseless when Trump returned to power. The infrastructure of repression was already in place: weakened faculty governance, a precarious academic workforce, a managerial class fluent in surveillance and compliance, and a culture that treated protest as a liability rather than a democratic right. Trump did not need to invent new mechanisms of control. He simply activated existing ones. Executive orders banning DEI, the weaponization of immigration law against student activists, the defunding of research, and the coercion of universities into ideological submission were all made possible by a system that had already abandoned its public commitments.

This is why the book's argument is so unsettling, and so important. It refuses the comforting fiction that universities are innocent victims of authoritarian power. It insists instead on reckoning with complicity, accommodation, and silence. Faculty who retreated into careerism, administrators who governed through fear and metrics, and governing boards who prioritized financial insulation over moral responsibility all helped produce the conditions in which higher education could be captured. The book does not moralize this history, but it does not excuse it either.

Yet, this is not a book of despair. It is a book of political clarity, and that clarity comes into sharp focus in its concluding chapter. There, the author shifts from diagnosis to demand, from exposure to responsibility. The final pages insist that critique alone is insufficient, and naming injustice without organizing against it merely reproduces the conditions of defeat. What is required instead is a renewed commitment to collective action, institutional courage, and the hard work of rebuilding higher education as a democratic commons.

The call to action advanced in the book's conclusion is both concrete and expansive. It urges faculty to reclaim shared governance not as a procedural formality but as a moral practice. It calls on unions to broaden their struggles beyond wages and contracts toward the defense of academic freedom, racial justice, and student rights. It challenges students to recognize themselves not as consumers navigating a credential marketplace, but as political agents capable of reshaping the institutions they inhabit. And it demands that administrators choose sides, either to continue managing decline in the service of power or to defend the university as a space of dissent, critical inquiry, and democratic possibility.

Readers should approach this book not as an insider's account of academic dysfunction, but as a warning and an invitation. What happens in universities does not stay in universities. The professionals, managers, policymakers, and cultural workers produced by these institutions shape every domain of social life, from law and medicine to policing, media, and governance. A higher education system that trains obedience rather than critical thought is a gift to authoritarian power. A higher education system reclaimed as a democratic public sphere can become one of the most powerful sites of resistance we possess.

Taken together, MAGAcademy demands that we abandon the fantasy that democracy can survive without democratic institutions, and that education can remain politically neutral in the face of rising authoritarianism. It reminds us that pedagogy is always political, that institutions teach by what they do as much as by what they claim, and that the struggle over higher education is inseparable from the struggle over the future itself.

This book deserves a wide readership, not only among educators and students, but among all those who believe that democracy requires more than empty slogans and managed dissent.

It offers clarity where confusion reigns, courage where fear has been normalized, and a language of resistance at a time when such language is being actively suppressed. Most importantly, it insists that the university can still matter, but only if we are willing to fight for it as a crucial site that both enables and defends democracy.

Preface

"Do you want a career in academia?" That was the first thing my trusted colleague asked after reading an early draft of this manuscript. She was not being hyperbolic: she was concerned that my personal story and critique would be weaponized against me in the so-called ivory tower. I got a chuckle out of it. However, her question forced me to confront a missing piece of the narrative: Why exactly did I write *MAGAcademy*? I wrote it because I am witnessing the collapse of the American university in real time, and I realized that to save it, we must first understand how we paved the road to our own undoing.

In the opening days of Donald Trump's second presidency, a chilling effect swept across academic institutions. It was a palpable fear that any student or faculty member might be disciplined, fired, or removed—violently or otherwise—for the simple act of critiquing the state of Israel. As budgets for critical research were slashed, campus leadership began to fold, surrendering to demands to purge any policy deemed "Diversity, Equity, and Inclusion (DEI) compliant." While I have long been a critic of corporate-led DEI initiatives because they tend to deliver on corporatism, not the promises or goals of DEI advocates, what Trump was doing was an equally blatant bait-and-switch. The eradication of DEI was not about fairness; it was about erasing the history and contributions of women, people of color, Indigenous people, and immigrants to make room for a mandated "patriotic education." Indeed, they were removing not just DEI policies, but curriculum that focused on the horrors of racist systems such as plantation slavery, as well as monuments dedicated to minorities.[1] As I watched campus executives surrender their academic freedom, I realized that the

MAGAcademy was no longer a mere threat—it had become our new reality.

My motivation for writing this book was to provide a directive on what to do should we ever get the chance to overturn this influence. History tells us that we cannot simply wait for the pendulum to swing back. When Trump took office in 2017, neoliberal Democrats dismissed his presidency as a fluke, operating under the assumption that they could simply reset the political clock to 2015 once they regained power. Democrats failed to realize that their neoliberal agenda—defined by corporatism and a hollowed-out 'center'—forged the very tools that enabled the rise of Trump's Make America Great Again (MAGA) agenda in the first place.

The neoliberal era marginalized a genuine revolutionary Left and replaced it with a reductive identitarianism. A vision of class solidarity was traded for an "Oppression Olympics." When the economic system failed during the Great Recession of 2008, neoliberal elites refused to change course. Unlike the 1930s, when the failure of laissez-faire capitalism gave rise to a new economic system known as the New Deal, the modern establishment doubled down on the failed system of neoliberalism. Barack Obama campaigned for the presidency in 2008 as an outsider but governed as a neoliberal insider, bailing out banks, insurance companies, and the airline industry while leaving workers to fend for themselves. This abandonment fueled the anger that Trump eventually tapped into. Even after the horrors of January 6th, 2021, when the contesting of the 2020 Presidential Election turned violent and deadly, the establishment held on to its crumbling agenda. At the helm sat an influential architect of neoliberalism, President Joe Biden, whose crippled economy, fixation on foreign entanglements, and decaying mental state paved the way for Trump's return to power.

When Trump took the reins again, he did not have to build a new apparatus of control; he simply weaponized the one the neoliberals left behind. Just as previous administrations used federal funding as a carrot to enforce identity policies, Trump used it as a stick to dismantle them. The neoliberal era normalized a culture of surveillance where people reported one another for bias; Trump merely incentivized reporting "anti-patriotism." Neoliberals' fetishization of corporate tech became Trump's fetishization of AI, and the long-standing bureaucratic war on faculty unions provided the perfect infrastructure for mass funding cuts.

My goal in writing *MAGAcademy* is to hold up a mirror to the processes that proud anti-MAGA liberals engaged in that made this MAGAcademy possible. We cannot continue making the same mistakes and expect different results. The critiques within this book have been whispered in faculty lounges for decades; my aim is to place them in a broader context to show exactly how we built the MAGAcademy. Only by acknowledging the failures of the past can we hope to build a future for higher education that is worth defending.

Paving the Road to the MAGAcademy

"People can have a difference of opinion." Farley, a gray-faced bureaucrat from the university's labor relations office, repeated the phrase for what felt like the tenth time in a twenty-minute meeting. He looked like an archetype of "the administrator" that modern universities fetishize: an overweight white man in a wrinkled white button-down shirt, glasses slipping down his nose, exuding the confidence of someone whose most radical undergraduate reading was probably scribbled in Sharpie on a bathroom stall.

What gnawed at me wasn't just the repetition, it was the categorical error. Farley was conflating opinion and argument, pretending they were interchangeable. Yes, people can have different opinions. But not every position is grounded in evidence, and not every perspective deserves equal weight. Not everyone has a compelling argument, as demonstrated by Farley.

What bothered me even more was that my training in a doctoral program for education managers had taught me the script that he was following: show up to "stakeholder" meetings, make faculty *feel* heard, but never actually listen, because faculty had little formal power. Farley was following the manual to the letter.

And here we were, the faculty labor representatives, meeting because the university had rolled out a new set of policies in response to student protests and encampments that were critical of

U.S. support for Israeli attacks on civilians in Gaza after October 7, 2023. The policies were conveniently drawn up while faculty were on summer break, and the new draconian rules effectively outlawed protest on campus. Practiced by generations of graduate and undergraduate students and constitutionally protected, student expression is as varied as departmental majors.[1]

Whether they are marches, sit-ins, vigils, or boycotts—celebratory or confrontational—their core purpose is to highlight glaring injustices and demand change. In the United States, the First Amendment explicitly protects the rights of students to protest by guaranteeing their freedoms of speech, assembly, and petition.[2] Although governments, and by extension administrators, can regulate the time, place, and manner of protests in order to allow the expression of even unpopular views, restrictions on them are legally mandated to be content-neutral. Courts consistently uphold such protests as central to democratic self-governance, and banning or dispersing them is permitted only under conditions defined as "clear and present danger." There are independent requirements that constitute such danger: one is the threat of serious harm that the government can prevent, and the other is a real and immediate danger.[3]

To justify the new policies, campus administrators cited unsubstantiated claims about how faculty and students felt "discomfort" with the activism. Dense layers of new restrictions on timing, where events could take place, and how loud they could be, sadly had the predictable effect—meaningful protest would be nearly impossible. It was a classic administrative tactic: weaponize social-justice language about caring, and the campus community, to mask a bureaucratic process built to restrict rights and silence dissent.

It was the fall term of 2024, and the protests of the previous spring had shaken the nation. Footage of police in riot gear confronting students on college campuses was broadcast across major news channels and widely circulated across social media platforms. Establishment media and political pundits conflated student protests against the Israeli government with antisemitism, providing a rhetorical weapon for the incoming Trump administration. But that administration was still months away. The assaults on constitutional rights on college campuses were happening under the leadership of the president and political party most people in higher education seemed to support: Joe Biden and the Democratic Party.[4]

Many of my colleagues accepted the prevailing propaganda about the activists and welcomed the crackdown on student and faculty rights. Their instinct to side with the Democratic Party and legacy news media's narratives—no matter the cost to collective bargaining power or faculty freedoms—was already a well-established pathology.

The meeting with Farley unfolded over Zoom, now the standard videoconferencing platform for labor disputes. Faculty union members occupied one side of the screen, while the administrators, including Farley, sat on the other. I was tasked with pleading our case to defend the rights of our labor union, students, and faculty. There I was, reduced to begging an administrator to respect rights that should never be negotiable in a university setting. The absurdity of having to plead for free expression spoke volumes about how bureaucrats, administrators, faculty, students, and everyday citizens had collectively allowed the crisis in higher education to metastasize.

My arguments were straightforward: protect constitutional rights rather than police political debate. But nothing landed. Farley wasn't there to consider policy; he was there to perform. I recognized the routine: nod gravely, feign thoughtful engagement, then walk away claiming, "We consulted with stakeholders and made the hard decision…" which always meant ignoring us.

And that's exactly what happened. Across the country, campuses were tightening the screws: debates were censored, speech was restricted, peaceful assembly was banned, and even email communication about protests was prohibited under the auspices of fighting hate. Faculty and students alike were being steamrolled by increasingly authoritarian administrations. It is a bitter irony: the very administrators who championed social justice as a bulwark against Trumpism were developing the infrastructure he would eventually use to transform the university into the MAGAcademy.

The Gaza protests revealed just how far the system had deteriorated: students and faculty were punished for engaging in the very forms of activism universities once claimed to champion. Administrators leaned on narrow interpretations of laws and campus policies and manufactured public fear to silence dissent, while too many faculty chose career preservation over principle.

The U.S. support for Israeli operations in Gaza and the clampdown on campus protest were not the root causes of the crisis. They merely exposed it as an increasingly transparent political agenda. Decades of neoliberal restructuring had already hollowed out the public mission of higher education, weakened collective bargaining power, eroded shared governance, undermined academic freedom, and transformed students into customers, all while deprofessionalizing faculty. Yes, flashpoint moments like Gaza, Trump's first election, and the Covid-19 pandemic accelerated these trends, but the decline had been underway for decades. All of this rot beneath the surface meant that when the real assault finally arrived, the system was too weak to withstand it.

From Neoliberal Drift to the MAGAcademy

Donald Trump's second term brought a coordinated, systematic campaign to transform higher education into what I call the MAGAcademy. The "MAGAcademy" is more than a play on words—it is a description of a new reality. It captures how Trump's "Make America Great Again" (MAGA) political movement reached beyond rhetoric to physically occupy the university, utilizing the infrastructure of neoliberal corporatism to install a new, authoritarian brand of campus life. Within weeks of returning to office in 2025, he issued sweeping executive orders banning diversity, equity, and inclusion (DEI) policies across all federal agencies, reversing Title IX protections for transgender students, and redefining sex strictly as male or female.[5] Campuses were stripped of their "sensitive location" status, clearing the way for immigration raids and arrests.[6] Federal agencies froze, canceled, or withdrew billions in grants and research contracts, most notably nearly $900 million from the Institute of Education Sciences, while the Office for Civil Rights was gutted and seven of its twelve regional branches eliminated.[7] By October 2025, the White House had sent ultimatums to nine major universities demanding that they implement a list of ideological conditions in exchange for continued access to federal funds. It was an unprecedented attempt to force political conformity onto higher education.[8]

The administration's crackdown extended far beyond institutions, sweeping up individual students and scholars in its dragnet. At Georgetown University, student activist Badar Khan Suri was detained and interrogated for organizing pro-Palestinian demonstrations, while at Columbia University, Mahmoud Khalil and Mohsen Mahdawi faced federal investigations that resulted in temporary detention and threats of imprisonment tied to alleged "material support" violations.[9] At Cornell University, student organizer Momodou Taal had his immigration status placed under review, putting him at risk of deportation.[10] Even international scholars were not spared: Turkish doctoral student Rümeysa Öztürk, a respected researcher affiliated with Columbia, had her visa abruptly revoked after participating in a campus teach-in; she was detained by ICE officers during a pre-dawn raid and was eventually expelled from the United States under the administration's newly expanded national-security authorities.[11] These cases illustrated the strategic precision of Trump's campaign, using the power of immigration law, criminal investigation, and federal surveillance to silence dissent, intimidate activists, and make examples of those who challenged the administration's narratives on Palestine, race, and academic freedom.

Certain institutions—most notably Harvard University and the Massachusetts Institute of Technology (MIT)—possessed the financial insulation necessary to resist, largely because their massive endowments shielded them from the threat of federal retaliation.[12] But most did not. To the shock of many, Columbia University and the University of California, Berkeley (UCB) capitulated, complying with federal demands.[13] The capitulation across the nation revealed that Trump had identified and exploited the weakness of higher education. These institutions had become obsessed with process and profit over people and principles. Trump's assault succeeded precisely because it operated through the bureaucratic machinery of corporatizing practices that administrators had spent decades perfecting. The neoliberal technocrats who had hollowed out higher education from within were losing power to the anti-intellectual authoritarians intent on destroying higher education.

The Roadmap:
From Institutional Decay to Radical Renewal

This book is about higher education: what it was supposed to be, what it evolved into, and how it became so profoundly vulnerable to the Trump Administration. Its central argument is simple: Trump did not mastermind the dismantling of American higher education. He merely exploited weaknesses that had been manufactured over generations by corporate-aligned administrators, complacent governing boards, and faculty who were often either disempowered or complicit. The same institutions that now claim to be "defending higher ed" against the MAGAcademy spent years laying the groundwork for its erosion. Worse, they built the very infrastructure Trump would later employ to build the MAGAcademy: undemocratic funding structures, the quiet erosion of civil liberties under the banner of "fighting hate," and the suppression of academic freedom in the name of "inclusion."

And while faculty and administrators fought bitterly among themselves over these issues, they shared one thing: a deep disdain for Trump and the MAGA movement. Yet, in a twist that should surprise no one, it was the neoliberal administrators, along with careerist faculty, who enabled them by creating and legitimizing a system perfectly primed for Trump's exploitation.

I know, because I watched it happen. I sat through the pointless committee meetings, the task forces, the retreats filled with corporate jargon, where administrators persuaded faculty to adopt policies openly hostile to the core principles of higher education once based on pedagogy, learning, and a meaningful education required for democratic citizenship. Faculty were far from blameless. Many part-time and contingent instructors –exploited laborers with few rights and little job security simply lacked the institutional power or protection to resist. But plenty of adjunct educators embraced the shift toward market logic, prioritizing "career readiness" and technological efficiency over critical inquiry and democratic responsibility. As a whole, tenured faculty, who had stronger protections in the profession, either were unable or declined to use their collective bargaining power (when they had it) to halt adjunctification, and some, in later years, became corporate professionals themselves, convinced that individual ladder-climbing would somehow advance the social justice goals once promised by the Marxists they long dismissed.

Administrators welcomed this shift. As part of the professional managerial class (PMC), they managed universities, public and private alike, as if they were for-profit corporations. Faculty were "workers" to be disciplined for the sake of accountability and efficiency; campuses were to be optimized for profiteering through data analytics; and the pursuit of knowledge was secondary to brand management. In fairness, they were following the agenda set by the politicians, boards of trustees, and regents, many drawn straight from industry and steeped in laissez-faire capitalist ideology. For them, decision-making revolved around liability and optics. Anything controversial, such as critical inquiry, had to be eliminated. Every institutional failure was treated as a public-relations problem. If rising tuition and declining academic standards created public backlash, they simply declared a renewed commitment to DEI or social justice and called it progress.

The casualties of these decisions are the generations that followed. Students were no longer viewed as future leaders in a democratic society but as customers. And "the customer is always right." Thus, the rise of "student-centered learning" in which feelings replaced knowledge and satisfaction surveys replaced intellectual rigor. Learning was less important than making sure students felt "supported" and "resilient," even if they graduated without the capacity for critical thought.

This was the system Trump encountered: a sprawling landscape of college graduates, including many faculty, who had been trained without deep critical inquiry, democratic values, or historical perspective; and a professoriate divided between exhausted faculty, upward-climbing corporatists, and demoralized idealists who had long abandoned hope of collective resistance. Administrators, fresh from watching neoliberal narratives on the Democratic Party–friendly MSNBC and clutching their "I'm With Her" bumper stickers from Hillary Clinton's 2016 presidential campaign, feigned shock as Trump dismantled the very system they had spent decades hollowing out. They pleaded with faculty and students they had routinely exploited to "stand with them" against Trump as governing boards capitulated to him, prioritizing financial and political interests over the public good.

I witnessed this collapse firsthand, as both a scholar and a participant. I have taught at community colleges, public universities, private institutions, and everything in between. I have seen the decay up close. I write this book as someone who still believes in the promise of higher education, and as someone who has watched that promise become steadily corrupted. My motivations are straightforward. Let me first correct the record: both the Left and the Right distort higher education in ways that mislead the public. Conservatives warn of campuses overrun by Marxist radicals, yet genuinely critical, inquiry-driven socialists are absent or severely marginalized at institutions. Liberals, meanwhile, cling to the fantasy that higher education remains a free, inclusive space for inquiry that empowers learners and scholars to transform our world toward social justice, but this conceals the for-profit corporatism in today's higher education, which runs counter to that narrative. These misleading interpretations are spread to the public by podcasters like Joe Rogan, comedians like Bill Maher, and social media political personalities like the late Charlie Kirk who portray today's students as dumb, hateful, and disengaged. Such narratives miss the point entirely. Students are not the problem. They are navigating a system that no longer resembles what it claims to be, and their frustration, confusion, and anger when that system does not deliver what it promised for them or society is rational and should be expected.

And if you think this story doesn't concern you because you're not on a campus, think again. The collapse of colleges and universities is not a contained institutional failure; it reverberates through every corner of what remains of our society.

Higher education increasingly produces a steady stream of market-driven, ladder-climbing professionals who fetishize management and executive authority. These are the people shaping, and in many cases undermining, our collective life—from government and the environment to public health, community, and civic belonging. Despite the rugged individualism that dominates U.S. rhetoric, our society depends on the competence, ethics, and judgment of one another.

We should seek an education system that produces people— politicians, soldiers, police officers, lawyers, judges, teachers, pilots, drivers, managers, trades people, hospitality workers, childcare workers, social workers, mental-health professionals, and countless others—who are guided by more than profit metrics and market incentives. Yet, the institutions responsible for their training increasingly teach them to prioritize revenue over responsibility, outcomes over ethics, rhetoric over reality, performative displays over meaningful skill development, and passing a course over learning, thereby obscuring the real harms their decisions can inflict.

My Journey Through the Collapse

This text is both memoir and manifesto. It blends history, political analysis, and frontline experiences from discussions with students and faculty in classrooms, faculty meetings, union halls, and campus protests. Each chapter anchors structural shifts in personal vignettes, revealing their human costs. Chapter One traces the corporatization of higher education, exploring how a sprawling professional managerial class has usurped power from faculty and students, prioritizing metrics and liability over scholarship and pedagogy. This erosion deepens in Chapter Two, where adjunctification and the devaluation of intellectual labor fragment faculty and reduce academic work to precarious service roles, undermining collective resistance and scholarly rigor. Chapter Three chronicles how the market logic that drives neoliberal managerialism recast students as customers. This resulted in generations of students burdened with debt and disillusioned by an anti-intellectual culture that prioritizes credentials over critical inquiry.

Building on these structural critiques, Chapter Four explains how campus culture experienced rapid erosion during Trump's first term, the Covid-19 pandemic, and the Gaza protests. This chapter explores neoliberal administrations' reliance on vapid rhetoric around social justice and DEI initiatives to stave off political backlash and public frustration. These performative tools for risk management and public relations, creating an environment of control and fragmentation rather than genuine democratic reform, left higher education vulnerable to exploitation by President Trump. Chapter

Five explores the way President Trump capitalized on faculty disempowerment and the profit- and process-oriented PMC to weaponize campus culture wars and bring about the MAGAcademy. In conclusion, Chapter Six offers a hopeful and pragmatic vision for reclaiming higher education as a democratic public good, emphasizing the restoration of faculty governance, reinvestment in academic labor, tuition-free education, and a recommitment to collective civic responsibility as essential steps toward rebuilding institutions capable of fostering critical thought, social justice, and democratic engagement.

Together, these chapters tell a cautionary tale: higher education did not transform into the MAGAcademy overnight. Its vulnerabilities were cultivated over decades, leaving it susceptible to exploitation by those seeking to weaken or manipulate it. Yet through historical analysis, personal narrative, and concrete examples of resistance, the book emphasizes that renewal is possible—and that reclaiming higher education requires collective action, principled leadership, and a refusal to accept market logic as destiny.

The Bureaucracy That Ate the University

It had been a long day, and I was fighting heavy eyelids as Sumayyah, a twenty-something-year-old student in my night class, sat down across the desk from me in my office. The class was set to begin in an hour. We had spoken briefly in class a few times, and she had noted that her family was from the Middle East. I didn't know if she was born abroad, but she had a thick accent.

I had started teaching the first of my courses that day at 8 a.m., and I was now preparing for my fifth course of the day, which was set to begin at 6 p.m. Even though I was exhausted, the night classes were my favorite. They were usually full of working professionals and night owls who were serious about completing their education and engaging with the subject matter. I also took great pride in bringing up the energy level for people who were as exhausted as I was at the end of the day.

Sumayyah made small talk about class and noted that she was having some difficulty keeping up with the reading. We were a few weeks into the course, and I had already noticed that Sumayyah had taken to the course material. For example, I remember her asking thoughtful questions during a lecture on the history of women being legally classified as property. Usually, students don't start coming to office hours until later in the term, when slipping grades begin to paint a bleak picture of their academic futures. Since Sumayyah was a good student and showed interest in the content, I assumed she was there to get a deeper understanding of the course content. That was not the case.

As Sumayyah spoke, I listened intently. She noted that she found it difficult to keep up with the course requirements because she had so many competing responsibilities at home. This part of the story is hard to explain, because it was less about what she said and more about how she said it. I sensed something was wrong. Maybe it was the long pauses, the refusal to make eye contact at certain times, or the disconnected stream of thought. Finally, I asked, "Is everything okay?"

"No," she replied, with tears starting to brim in her eyes. She explained that her husband was unhappy about her attending school. He had only allowed her to pursue an education so long as it did not interfere with *her* domestic duties. Three hours of my class a week on top of homework and whatever other courses she was taking had made it impossible for her to have dinner ready for him—*on time*. She consistently cited her "culture" as the reason he expected her to behave that way and said I probably didn't understand because it's not my "culture."

She was upset, and again, I sensed there was more beneath the surface. So, I asked gently, "If you don't mind me asking, and you don't have to share, is it just that he's getting angry, or is something else going on?"

In a disjointed way, as only someone suffering abuse can convey, she indicated, but did not directly say it was both physical and emotional. My heart sank. I stayed quiet, letting her speak. For a moment, I thought of a middle-school classmate I had once seen abused by her father. Back then, I told her friend about it, but not an adult. I have regretted my inaction ever since, and the memory flashed through me with sudden clarity. But I reminded myself: This wasn't about me. This was about her.

As I began to say, "You know no one should treat you that way, right?" my training kicked in. Not training in how to help a victim of abuse, but the bureaucratic training I had received in graduate school: the mandate to interrupt and say, "I am a court-mandated reporter." Essentially, I had to inform her that if she told me about criminal abuse, I was required to report it to my superiors. I did not directly remind her that I was a court-mandated reporter but instead suggested that I reach out to my manager to see what support we could provide.

Her expression shifted to terror. She begged me not to report it. I agreed not to use her name, saying I would only explore options with my manager. I told her she could skip class for the evening, and if she needed to, she could check in with me before the next class to compare notes so she wouldn't fall behind. She begged me not to email her about it, since her husband read her emails. I agreed.

The next day, I met with my manager and shared the story. He brought in another manager and a counselor. They told me I had handled everything correctly. Then the conversation took a turn. They began asking, "Were you alone in your office with her? Could anyone see inside, or was it visibly concealed?" I explained that yes, we were alone, but my door is essentially a giant window, so anyone could see into the office. I asked why that mattered. They explained, "We're trying to protect you." They said sometimes, in situations like this, victims might later accuse the person they confided in of something, out of fear or desire for self-preservation. In that moment, it became clear: the mandatory reporting system was not designed to protect the student, or even me; it was designed to protect the institution from liability.

Sumayyah never came back to class. I sent a few neutral emails but never heard from her again. Her situation still haunts me. I've replayed it a million times, wondering what I could have done differently. What stayed with me, too, was the anger—anger that the campus was primarily concerned with shielding itself and its white male professor, while the abused woman became a target of suspicion rather than someone deserving protection. I learned my lesson: serving students happens in spite of bureaucracy, not because of it.

A few years later, on the first day of another night class, I put students into groups and encouraged them to exchange contact information. After a break, while I was droning on about syllabus policies, I noticed two women staring at their phones, their expressions resembling nervous laughter. I asked what was going on.

One student (let's call her Tina) explained: "Our group exchanged phone numbers. During break, I mentioned I was getting married. One of the guys in the group didn't take it well. He stomped off shouting 'I fucking hate married women!' and then started sending me texts saying he was going to kill me and my fiancé."

She read the messages aloud. The class froze. What started as awkward laughter over his tantrum quickly morphed into fear.

This time, I mentioned the mandated reporting requirement but decided not to leave it at that. I told the class I'd walk with Tina to campus police and welcomed anyone who wanted to join. That way, there would be a police report documenting the incident with witnesses to support the account. If necessary, I thought, I could involve the student newspaper to elevate the issue and push for justice.

This time, the campus took action. Citing the threatening texts, they removed the student from campus and barred him from returning. Our class was moved to a new location. Tina finished the course with an A. Last I heard, her life was going well.

. Universities often rely on a wide array of administrative measures—ranging from student evaluations to mandatory trainings on sexual harassment, cybersecurity, diversity, and inclusion—which they present as tools for strengthening the campus community and enhancing learning. In practice, however, they do the opposite. They do not solve real problems, but create the appearance of safety, equity, and accountability.

This is because the real goal of the institution, from the perspective of the trustees, managers, and executive officers, is to turn a profit. Like any corporation, these institutions of higher education see the economic cost of such incidents rather than the impact they have on the humans in the institution. But it was not always this way.

In this chapter, I show how the corporatist approach to education that emerged in the 1970s, known as neoliberalism, transformed higher education by turning over what was once a public good to a private for-profit system. This chapter unpacks the ways neoliberal ideology, far from the progressive or leftist ideal many assume, has colonized the university, replacing intellectual rigor with corporate managerialism and causing the expansion of non-teaching manager and staff positions known as administrative bloat. It is this neoliberal logic, more than any outside attack, that hollowed out higher education. Understanding this origin and logic of neoliberalism provides the scaffolding and context for examining the downfall of education and the broader social landscape explored in this book.

Neoliberalism

Neoliberalism is essentially a rebranding of the 18th- and 19th-century Western economic model known as laissez-faire capitalism, a system ultimately abandoned in the early 20th century after it fueled massive wealth disparities and helped enable authoritarian regimes.[1] Laissez-faire capitalism is an economic system defined by minimal government intervention, limited mostly to protecting big business, based on the belief that what benefits business ultimately benefits the entire economy.[2] Proponents champion free markets, private property rights, and self-regulation through supply and demand, trusting that individual self-interest, guided by the "invisible hand," will correct market imbalances and benefit all, so long as government, even when well-intentioned, stays out of economic affairs.[3]

Laissez-faire capitalism was largely abandoned after its contribution to the Great Depression and the subsequent rise of totalitarian regimes. In its wake, a system of managed economic policy emerged, known internationally as Keynesian economics and in the United States as New Deal Liberalism.[4] At its heart, New Deal Liberalism represented a new social contract: the belief that a stable democracy required a regulated market, strong labor protections, and a robust social safety net to shield citizens from the inherent volatility of capitalism. By the 1970s, Keynesian models fell out of favor amid economic crises like stagflation and a broader public distrust in government fueled by scandals such as Watergate and revelations from the Church Committee hearings.[5] In its place, a new economic and political logic emerged: neoliberalism.

From Jimmy Carter to Joe Biden, every subsequent president has embraced neoliberal logic to varying degrees.[6] This was no random transition, but a highly organized one. Its blueprint was the 1971 "Powell Memo," a confidential call to arms written by future Supreme Court Justice Lewis F. Powell Jr. for the U.S. Chamber of Commerce—a powerful business federation dedicated to pro-business advocacy and economic growth. Powell urged corporate America to move beyond passive lobbying and instead launch a coordinated, aggressive assault on the institutions shaping public thought: specifically, media, academia, politics, and the judiciary. The goal was to mobilize business leaders to protect corporate power and shift the political landscape away from the 1970s-era support for government regulation. Over the following decades, this mandate was operationalized through massive corporate funding, transforming the university from a site of public inquiry into a laboratory for neoliberal policy and culture.[7]

Neoliberalism operates on the assumption that government is inherently corrupt, market intervention is harmful, and public-sector workers and unions are obstacles to efficiency. Its solution is to manage public institutions like corporations, prioritizing profit and market metrics in systems originally designed to serve people rather than shareholders.[8] While neoliberals contend that their approach can deliver the material abundance, social stability, and peace that Marxism only theorized, critics argue that these laissez-faire roots leave nations vulnerable to the same catastrophic outcomes that marked the early 20th century: depressions and authoritarian regimes. In *The Capital Order*, Clara Mattei argues that neoliberalism aims to replace the political left—including socialists, communists, and anarchists—with centrist alternatives. This strategy is inherently dangerous because, as demonstrated in the 1930s, when the political center loses support during economic crises—such as the Great Depression, the 2008 Great Recession, or the Covid-19 pandemic—the public is often left with only one perceived alternative: the authoritarian right.[9]

Corporatizing the University

Neoliberalism's ascendancy transferred wealth and power from public institutions to the corporate sector, profoundly reshaping education.[10] Neoliberals argued that corporations are more efficient because they face accountability mechanisms that public institutions lack. As a result, public education became a primary target for neoliberal restructuring. The shift aimed to diminish faculty power, historically focused on scholarship, teaching, and the public good, in favor of corporate interests emphasizing profits, global competitiveness, and workforce development.

The Schools are Failing!
The corporatization driven by neoliberalism was justified by two factors. The first was the belief that schools were failing to educate students and the nation was suffering as a result. This conclusion was drawn by a 1983 report from President Ronald Reagan's administration titled *A Nation at Risk*. The report claimed public schools were failing the nation's economy and global competitiveness.[11] Although the report was flawed and contradicted by contemporary studies, conservative policy-makers embraced it to justify reforms such as Head Start, No Child Left Behind, and Common Core.[12] These policies epitomized corporate logic as they emphasized standardized testing and data-driven accountability,

rewarding well-performing schools with more funding while punishing underfunded ones, exacerbating inequalities rather than averting them.[13] Standardized tests are poor measures of a school's effectiveness, because they assess memorization rather than genuine learning or critical thinking.[14] They ignore students' life circumstances and community factors. Worse, they diminish education by reducing it to rote memorization and bubble filling, producing individuals who can find the right answer but lack critical thinking skills.[15]

Nonetheless, enough of the public bought into this narrative that voting patterns began to shift, leading many to support politicians who promised greater fiscal responsibility and government accountability. In states like California, voters backed legislation such as Proposition 13, which drastically reduced property taxes and consequently slashed revenue for public services, including schools.[16] At both the state and national levels, politicians, most notably Reagan, popularized austerity measures, policies aimed at reducing budget deficits and public debt through spending cuts, under the promise that doing so would stabilize the economy.[17]

Supporters frequently cite the 230 percent increase in government funding for public education between 1960 and 2020 as evidence of sustained public investment.[18] Yet this argument obscures the uneven distribution of those resources. Funding was disproportionately concentrated in affluent districts, thereby exacerbating preexisting patterns of economic inequality.[19] Relatedly, as public services like mental health and food assistance were phased out due to tax cuts, higher education institutions stepped in to fill the void.[20] Consequently, universities assumed an expanding array of functions, necessitating the development of extensive administrative bureaucracies. Although federal aid increased during this period, it failed to keep pace with escalating tuition costs, revenues that administrators increasingly depended upon to finance the continued growth of these bureaucratic structures.[21]

Globalize the Economy

The second factor justifying the corporatization of education was globalization. Comprising the rapid acceleration and magnitude of transnational exchange, including goods, services, technology, investment, and migration, globalization signifies the increasing integration of distinct national economies and societies into a shared, interdependent global system, thereby fostering greater interaction between diverse populations and cultures. By the late 1990s, global capitalism was touted by neoliberals as an inevitable outcome of the Cold War, which ended in 1991 with the fall of the Soviet Union. In 1997, Bill Readings argued in *The University in Ruins* that universities could no longer protect national culture amid declining nation-states; they had to embrace globalization. In practice, this meant creating a more corporate-friendly landscape at home and abroad. Louis Menand described this vision in *The New Yorker* as deregulation, tax cuts for the wealthy, and a focus on market efficiency over public welfare.[22] While globalization was touted by U.S. lawmakers as lifting billions worldwide from poverty, it entrenched inequality domestically, destabilizing democracy. For example, CEO pay in the U.S. skyrocketed from forty-two times the average employee's salary in 1980 to 347 times in 2016, while the wealthiest one percent of Americans now collectively owns more than the bottom 90 percent.[23]

Neoliberals proposed education as the remedy for poverty, urging all Americans to become white-collar workers through college degree attainment. President Clinton asserted this with his famous aphorism "We live in a world in which what you earn depends on what you can learn."[24] Instead of making college tuition-free, a government intervention neoliberals oppose, citizens were offered student loans to finance their education. The idea was that those in poverty would face a reduction in public services, but if they made it to college age, they would be able to take on massive amounts of debt for the opportunity to attain a college degree. The federal government had been making some student loans available to citizens since the 1950s. However, access to student loans—and the debt it engenders—was expanded with the Higher Education Amendments of 1992, which broadened eligibility and access for federal loans while raising the annual loan limits.[25] Student loan debt in the U.S. rose from $24 billion in 1990–91 to $1.75 trillion in 2024.[26] In 2025, the average federal student loan debt was $39,075 per borrower.[27] To make matters worse, in an effort led by then-Senator Joe Biden, the federal government banned student loans from being treated like other debts, which could be eradicated through bankruptcy.[28]

By the late 20th century, neoliberal budgets, now collecting less tax revenue, saw massive cuts to federal funding of social programs. State and local governments responded to shrinking budgets by freezing or reducing salaries and slashing programs at schools. At the same time, they relied on a reduced budget to provide services previously supported by federal funding, such as food assistance, housing relief, and mental health care.

Professional Managerial Class Vs. Faculty

A core neoliberal argument posited that to improve education, institutions need leaders with a business- or industry-oriented mindset. They argued that the private sector inherently possesses superior efficiency and accountability because its existence is fundamentally tied to profitability. Faced with budget crises from decades of disinvestment, institutions adopted corporate management styles, rebranding budget optimization and faculty accountability as their primary goals. As a result, neoliberal policymakers successfully advocated for the transformation of higher education into a corporate hierarchy that still exists today. This change effectively centralized fiduciary authority in the executive offices of presidents, chancellors, and boards of trustees, which are typically composed of wealthy donors, alumni, and politically connected appointees.[29]

To ensure the executive vision shapes education, faculty are minimized or removed from the decision-making process and replaced with members of the professional managerial class (PMC).[30] The PMC consists of middle-class professionals distinguished by above-average incomes and advanced education and training, often business qualifications or university degrees, who hold roles that entail societal influence typically reserved for capital owners.[31] Detractors of the PMC in education, such as University of California's Catherine Liu, characterize the PMC as affluent or white-collar left liberals plagued by a patronizing air toward the common, everyday laborers and their families.[32] At the behest of executives, the PMC bases its decision-making on collective data analysis.

The supremacy of the PMC in higher education was made possible by the reduction in faculty power, because, in the neoliberal view, faculty have historically held too much influence in higher education. Thus, for decades, under the rationale of fiscal responsibility in response to shrinking budgets, well-paid tenure-track (TT) faculty with strong benefits were replaced by lower-cost non-tenure-track and part-time (NTPT) faculty who receive few or no benefits and can be dismissed without cause, making them more compliant due to fear of losing their jobs.

In addition to weakening faculty power, the PMC's influence over campus life was reinforced through hiring practices such as the diversity statement. A diversity statement is an application requirement intended to assess an applicant's understanding of, experience with, and future plans for contributing to a more inclusive and equitable campus community. Although the diversity statement was introduced as a tool for identifying individuals committed to diversifying the institution, in practice it often functioned as a mechanism for enforcing ideological homogeneity. A 2022 study from the Foundation for Individual Rights and Expression (FIRE) found that half of the faculty surveyed identified as liberal, while 17 percent identified as moderate, and just over one-quarter (26 percent) identified as conservative.[33] Meanwhile, institutions such as Duke University and Harvard University report that approximately 60 percent and 80 percent of their faculty, respectively, identify as liberal.[34] The studies show that only about 10 percent of faculty identify as far-left, meaning that the overwhelming majority of the campus faculty are centrist neoliberals and conservatives, both of whom welcome the corporatist approach to education.[35]

Profit Over the Public Good

Neoliberal governance refashioned colleges and universities along corporate lines, prioritizing risk-taking, cost-cutting, and market-driven revenue over the public good.[36] As Christopher Newfield points out in *The Great Mistake*, market-driven demands for accountability and efficiency undermined higher education's ability to fulfill its obligation to serve the public good.[37] The public good captures the many ways higher education benefits society as a whole, from producing knowledgeable citizens to advancing innovation, culture, the economy, and democratic participation.

The PMC shifted institutions' focus to financialized growth models that relied on real estate development, auxiliary services, and debt-financed expansion.[38] This creates a feedback loop: universities raise tuition to pay bond debts tied to real estate and facilities expansions, which in turn justifies cutting faculty wages and reducing academic spending. Davarian L. Baldwin's *In the Shadow of the Ivory Tower* argues this financialized model constitutes a form of plunder, extracting wealth from students, faculty, and communities alike, undermining the democratic and civic purpose of higher education, and demanding urgent reevaluation of university budgeting, governance, and accountability.

As institutions shifted toward a market-driven model, they not only abandoned the public good but, at times, actively worked against it. For example, the Bayh-Dole Act of 1980 transformed the landscape of academic research by granting institutions the right to retain ownership of inventions developed with federal funding, rather than the federal government owning them.[39] It significantly incentivized corporations to partner with universities by allowing them to license and commercialize federally funded inventions, creating a clear path for private-sector investment, new companies (spin-offs), and economic growth, moving away from a system in which the government held most patents. By giving universities (and small businesses) ownership of these patents, the Act encouraged them to actively seek industry partners to develop and bring innovations to market, benefiting both academia and industry with royalties and returns on investment.[40] Historically, markets would typically avoid risk, while governments would assume major risks for national projects like the internet, railroads, highways, and the Apollo moon missions.[41] The Bayh-Dole Act shifted research toward projects promising immediate economic payoff, often at the expense of research with lasting public value.

As universities began functioning as landlords, developers, and asset managers, they pushed the costs of austerity not only onto students and faculty, but onto the surrounding communities as well. Baldwin argues that universities leverage their tax-exempt status to acquire vast real estate holdings and reshape surrounding communities into "UniverCities."[42] The term reveals that modern universities act as dominant economic and social forces, like "company towns" with their own budgets, governance, and law enforcement. This corporate-style management shifts public responsibilities onto surrounding marginalized neighborhoods, driving gentrification, displacement, and higher local costs.

Corporatization also engendered public distrust of higher education. In *Crisis in the Academy* (1998), Christopher Lucas argues that neoliberal reforms produced public confusion and skepticism about the institution's purpose.[43] Rather than addressing this tension by unequivocally declaring that they serve the public good or the market, universities have often resorted to public relations campaigns promoting themselves as "all things to all people," a strategy Lucas warns leads to "public distrust" when the university inevitably fails to fulfill all these roles. Compounding matters, corporatization of higher education has led to high-profile private-sector-esque scandals, such as former NFL quarterback Brett Favre's involvement in a university welfare fraud case; Tim Leiweke, former CEO of a commercial real estate firm, being charged with fraud for rigging bidding processes for university stadiums; and the Varsity Blues scandal, in which wealthy parents paid to secure their children's admission to elite schools.[44]

The Corporate Bureaucracy

If neoliberalism redesigned universities along corporate lines, bureaucracy is the machinery that keeps those institutions running, expanding, and justifying themselves. What emerges is a world in which process becomes the purpose: procedures displace judgment, performance replaces substance, and managerial rituals masquerade as accountability. The result is a university culture that is not radical but unmistakably liberal in the neoliberal sense, committed not to redistributive change or genuine justice but to the endless defense of procedures, workflows, compliance, and "best practices." This bureaucratic ethos shapes everything from hiring and evaluation to language, meetings, training, and even the meaning of safety itself, revealing a system that grows more sprawling and self-referential while steadily eroding university's intellectual and democratic mission.

When Process Becomes the Purpose
The dominance of neoliberalism in higher education helps explain both the creation and the defense of bureaucracy in the academy. Neoliberalism departs from the Left in that it is obsessed with maintaining and defending processes, even when those processes fail to deliver real results for people.[45] Process is to bureaucracy what doctrine is to religion. Bureaucracy is a term that refers to a system

of organization structured around rules, procedures, and hierarchical authority.[46] Sociologist Max Weber argued that bureaucracies are rational ways of dividing work into smaller, more manageable units.[47] In higher education this means that when a new policy is developed, an office or division is often created to oversee it. When one of these smaller offices struggles to manage its workload, it will be divided up, creating a new office with additional positions to share the burden. Over the decades, the result has been the expansion of layer upon layer of a sprawling administrative apparatus, staffed by people who are not faculty.

Such expansion was justified as a means to improve quality and accountability, but it came at a hidden cost. Every new office, policy, and reporting requirement added layers of work for faculty, usually without additional compensation or recognition. It has transformed faculty life into a cycle of paperwork: forms, training courses, evaluations, reporting. We become bureaucrats in our own classrooms, performing compliance instead of teaching. For example, the offices that provide students with accommodations, sometimes called disability resources offices, make recommendations on behalf of the campus regarding support services or classroom adjustments the faculty need to make in order to serve the particular needs of a student or students.

If faculty members disagree with a mandate, they must either expend the labor to restructure their course or engage in a formal debate with the accommodations office. In the latter case, they are required to demonstrate that the requested modification would compromise the learning environment for every student enrolled. The core of the issue is that many of these accommodations are designed by non-educators and, consequently, are aimed at helping students pass rather than learn. These measures often include granting a student unlimited time for exams or—unlike their peers— allowing them access to notes and textbooks during the test. Faculty are thus forced to choose between the administrative burden of facilitating alternative testing environments or engaging in an uphill battle with the accommodations office.

Even the use of technology creates work for faculty while reducing tasks for the bureaucracy. For example, students used to deliver their accommodation letters to faculty and discuss the accommodations. Now, the accommodation office sends a separate email for every student, and faculty are expected to sign in separately to approve or dispute each student accommodation. If there is an exam involved, some campuses require faculty to upload the same exam into the accommodation portal for each student. Similarly, ordering books, for instance, used to be as simple as one call or email to the campus bookstore saying, "I'm using the same texts as last term." Now, faculty must navigate a digital order form from a third-party company filled with prompts requesting more details—title, author, years, ISBN number, publishers —than are actually needed to identify the book. Emails from various offices are sent to faculty with the assumption that they are read. At one campus, a lengthy email announced that offices would need to be cleared for recarpeting, a few days before winter break. Many faculty did not have time to read it amid the 500 emails they receive daily, and their belongings were left outside in the rain. This bureaucratic creep occurs in small, seemingly quick tasks, but when added up, 40 to 50 each term, the impact is significant.

The ultimate result is an increase in labor and a drain on time, all without additional compensation. This reflects a profound and systemic misalignment between the professional mission of a professor and the bureaucratic reality of the modern university. Instead of acting as scholars dedicated to the pursuit of knowledge and the cultivation of students, faculty are increasingly coerced into wasting their intellectual capital on perfunctory, administrative tasks. These hollow requirements now dominate the majority of the workload, effectively cannibalizing the time that should be reserved for producing new research or fostering genuine student growth.

This is especially true for annual training courses. Depending on the institution, campuses may require yearly completion of courses on topics such as sexual harassment, anti-racism, cybersecurity, and more. These training courses, which can last anywhere from 30 minutes to two hours, are completed online. The timer only continues running while your cursor remains active on the training screen. As a result, even if you have taken the training multiple times and already know the material, you still must spend this time clicking through the modules instead of attending to other job responsibilities. NTPT faculty, who teach at multiple institutions, must complete four or five similar training courses every year at each campus.

Research has found that these trainings are often "cartoonish" in nature, primarily designed to protect institutions rather than produce measurable results in addressing the issues they claim to solve.[48] For example, at one of my former campuses, a professor of color was treated as a promotional prop for the mostly white school to signal its commitment to racial progress. He had served on the campus for years, which means he presumably had to complete the annual training on sexual violence and harassment. Tragically, this professor later plead guilty to charges related to the sex trafficking of a student. It is a sobering reminder that symbolic appointments and standard compliance training are not a substitute for rigorous accountability and genuine safety measures.

What administrators describe as "efficiency" often produces inefficiency, consuming hours of faculty time while leaving the core work of teaching largely untouched. The irony is sharp: institutions preach "student-centered learning" while redirecting faculty energy toward managerial busywork that erodes instructional quality. Students feel it, too. Time spent on forms is time not spent mentoring, giving feedback, or designing creative pedagogy. Classrooms become exercises in fulfilling administrative expectations rather than cultivating curiosity or critical thinking.

The Self-Preserving Bureaucracy

Bureaucracy is inherently self-preserving, and in higher education, its preservation relies on institutional processes that undermines knowledge production through incoherent directives and redefines scholars, thinkers, and educators as task-completing functionaries. Consider the evaluation process, in which one faculty member evaluates another alongside an administrator to determine whether they continue to meet the department's standards in teaching or scholarship. Although framed as supportive, these evaluations are structurally compelled to identify "areas for improvement," because identifying flaws legitimizes the administrative apparatus. A former department chair once told me that on numerous occasions he submitted a truly exemplary evaluation for a colleague, only to have it returned with instructions to find something, anything, that could be marked as needing improvement. After all, if faculty are doing their jobs well and independently, why would administrators be necessary?

Another method of expanding the bureaucracy is to take real problems, such as the persistent treatment of historically marginalized communities, and propose corporate solutions that empower the bureaucracy and weaken faculty, while failing to achieve the stated goal. This is certainly the case with campus commitments to diversity, equity, and inclusion (DEI). If campuses are serving the public good, they should be fostering DEI, but fostering is different than paying lip service.

Over the past two decades, universities have positioned themselves as champions of social justice by hiring large staffs and implementing policies like mandatory trainings, anti-racism committees, bias-reporting systems, and diverse hiring practices. Despite the high costs, there is little data proving these efforts achieve their stated goals.[49] DEI policies have been linked to improved retention and completion rates among historically marginalized communities; however, most studies focus on specific institutions or programs and report only modest gains.[50] It is common in DEI scholarship to admit that the successes have been few and far between. In the third edition of Kofi Lomotey and William A. Smith's *The Racial Crisis in American Higher Education*, they bemoaned the fact that "we find ourselves once again on a journey" of "social and economic distress, and racial and cultural animus."[51] They point out that the crisis DEI aims to address, remains. Similarly, in 2019 the American Council on Education tacitly admitted that DEI in education would need "redoubling" as they had failed to significantly diversify faculty at a time when over three-fourths of faculty identified as white, while Black, Latinx, and Native American faculty were collectively under-represented at 11 percent of full-time faculty.[52] Worse, some DEI initiatives can backfire. Rather than produce an inclusive environment, studies show, mandatory trainings can engender a sense of discomfort and unfairness that triggers a backlash of increased racial resentment.[53] Corporate approaches avoid providing direct economic help to historically marginalized identities, even though studies from both the Urban Institute and the Brookings Institution have found that kind of support would reduce inequality.[54] Direct economic assistance, however, would require taxing powerful corporations, which neoliberals see as verboten.

Bureaucratic Language and the Death of Meaning
Bureaucracies in higher education maintain power by creating new languages and stripping words of their original meaning. In *The Utopia of Rules: On Technology, Stupidity, and the Secret Joys of Bureaucracy* (2015), anthropologist David Graeber argues that bureaucracies impose "order" and "regularity" not to serve people, but to suppress creativity, turning language into a tool of control.[55] Bureaucratic language fractures comprehension rather than enabling communication. This is especially true in higher education. Contrary to the caricature painted by the Right, faculty lounges aren't filled with Marxist professors speaking in dense, revolutionary jargon. Instead, the campus soundscape is increasingly polluted by vapid

corporate talking points. Rather than deep, meaningful analysis, faculty are bombarded with hollow slogans. For example: "We need to encourage a warm hand off in our public facing documents as it has been shown to be the best practice for engendering retention and student success." In this kind of administrator jargon, buzzwords like "best practices," "warm hand offs," "public facing materials," and "student success" become common refrains from the managers and staff that comprise the bureaucratic administration. Faculty, meanwhile, roll their eyes, because they know the language is vapid rhetoric. A prime example is "student success," which colleagues, deans, researchers, and mentors have all admitted to me does not have a widely accepted meaning. The public is aware as well, as evidenced by widely followed social media accounts such as "Shit Management Says" emulating the empty rhetoric of neoliberal managers.[56] The result is that all terms become contested. Even ones that were previously well-defined, such as "social justice" and "academic freedom," are up for debate.

In practice, this produces a lexicon of inauthentic, nonsensical jargon, phrases designed to be measurable, evaluable, and safely recycled by process-oriented bureaucrats. These include a legion of absurd managerial titles. The *Hechinger Report* once compiled some of the most bizarre examples:[57]

> Assistant director of affinity group leadership (University of Denver)
> Constituent relationship management program manager (University of Massachusetts, Boston)
> Educational talent search academic advisor (Harris Stowe State University)
> Early career readiness and student employment program coordinator (University of Arizona)
> Coordinator of community standards (Governors State University)
> Academic success coordinator for peer-led instruction (Framingham State University)

Student involvement coordinator (North Carolina State
University)
Senior associate director of student engagement (Columbia
University)
Manager of employee communication and engagement
(Seminole State College)
Assistant director of admission student volunteers
(University of Pennsylvania)
Associate director of student conduct and community
standards (University of Tennessee at Knoxville)
Director of institutional effectiveness (Wabash College)
Customer relationship management coordinator (University
of Cincinnati)
Student journals and competitions coordinator (University of
Colorado)
Student philanthropy manager (University of California,
Berkeley)
Associate director of young alumni engagement (Kenyon
College)
Assistant director for athletic event and guest services
(Miami University)
Senior user experience analyst (University of Maryland
University College)
Vice president for planning, analytics, and decision support
(New York Institute of Technology)
Director of campus relations (University of Maryland)
Office concierge (University of Maryland University
College)

The list goes on, with each title more meaningless than the last. No
wonder internet pranksters created an "administrator title generator"
that went viral online.[58] Most rational people can see the futility and
humor of managerial language co-optation, but faculty must operate
in a space that pretends it is legitimate.

The consequences of this self-preserving bureaucracy extend far beyond administrative bloat. As empty language becomes institutional norm, critical concepts collapse into slogans, and decision-making in higher education grows unmoored from facts, reason, and debate. This is relativism in its institutional form: truth becomes whatever one feels, and competing facts become irrelevant. In place of rigorous argumentation, the core mission of education, administrators convene elaborate performances in which the goal is to sound intelligent, socially conscious, and "aligned" with institutional values while saying nothing substantive.

What does this look like in practice? Picture attending a meeting of the committee that reports to another committee, an all-too-real feature of contemporary academia. Faculty are summoned by the Dean of Hangnail Trauma for a mandatory "open dialogue" on "best practices" to address vaguely defined "challenges" that allegedly threaten the institution's "public-facing matrix," a matrix, of course, produced by a "cross-collaboration task force" of "relevant stakeholders" invested in "student success" and animated by the logic of "warm hand offs" that uphold our "DEI policies" for our "BIPOC (Black, Indigenous, and People of Color)" communities. Cue the inevitable land acknowledgment, delivered by the administrator eager to earn social-justice credibility by performatively atoning for their "privilege," "As a white person, I feel ashamed of what happened on this land. But as a leader, I take full responsibility. I will now read this acknowledgment to atone, even though I have no intention of returning the land."

Conclusion

Most tragically, those the system claims to protect, such as Sumayyah, are often the most burdened by it. Students are lost in a maze of paperwork and procedures. Bureaucracy that should be a safety net becomes a series of hurdles, compounding vulnerability rather than alleviating it. What emerges is a hollow theater of protection. Institutions design elaborate performances, trainings, checklists, and forms so that when harm occurs, they can point to the paperwork and say, "We tried."

Higher education bureaucracy is not broken; it functions precisely the way neoliberalism designed it to. Its primary aim is to protect the institution, often at the expense of students and faculty. Policies, training courses, and evaluations serve less to enhance learning and more to create an illusion of order that conceals systemic chaos, vulnerability, and human harm. In this system, procedures routinely trump people, compliance replaces creativity, and box checking has become the dominant curriculum. Faculty find themselves trapped in endless cycles of managerial ritual rather than meaningful teaching or deep scholarship, while students navigate complex bureaucratic mazes instead of thriving in environments meant to foster intellectual growth.

These experiences reveal a fundamental truth: the primary obstacle to learning and scholarly inquiry is not individual failings or poor pedagogy, but the bureaucratic apparatus itself, meticulously engineered to appear productive while accomplishing little of substantive value. The expansion of this apparatus is fueled by neoliberal logic, which cloaks institutional growth in rhetoric around equity, safety, and accountability, even as it hollows out academic freedom and intellectual rigor for faculty. And that is the subject of the next chapter.

From Scholar to Service Provider

"That is why I have the tenure-track job, and you are just an adjunct. They wanted me to have this position," spat the angry voice on the other end of the phone. It was a tenured colleague, Napoleon. I rolled my eyes, all too familiar with how tenured colleagues' resentment over my success had twisted into venomous words and petty maneuvers, desperate attempts to prove their worth in the face of an adjunct who outshone them at one turn or another. By this point in my career, I had become accustomed to this abusive form of elitism.

When I was younger, I might have snapped and said something cutting. But now, I was confident, tired, and indifferent. I learned to find humor in the absurdity of human behavior, especially in academia. After all, Napoleon, a journalism professor, was bragging about getting a job I hadn't even applied for. What could I do but smirk? After all, he clearly decided to call me and yell at me to make himself feel better.

This was far from the last time he would direct such vitriol toward me. A year later, he leveled another sharp rebuke via email— all because I had misplaced a single letter in his name. The disproportionate scale of his rage over a minor typo revealed a profound fragility, as if a misspelled name were a direct assault on his status. I chose to ignore his angry reply and instead wait for an opportunity to misspell his name again. Was it petty? Absolutely, but this profession has a way of making people petty. For example, a faculty member hated their college president so badly that they took their trash, from their home, to work every day and dumped it in the dumpster outside the president's window.

On the phone call, Napoleon's rage stemmed from what he considered a major offense: I had pointed out an error he made, and how it was negatively impacting our department. Twice before the term began, I asked him to meet with me to discuss the best way to have students' work submitted to the campus newspaper. That was a goal of the department. However, he brushed me off, saying we could "figure it out in Fall." He was tenured, which meant summers off. I wasn't so lucky. Since 2012, I've never taught less than a full-time summer load. When fall came, I started sending the newspaper my students' work. Weeks passed and nothing appeared. Napoleon did not have a system in place to analyze student work for publication. When I asked him about it, he grew flustered and lashed out, refusing to accept responsibility as the lead faculty for what had become a failed system. I hadn't criticized him personally, but it was enough to set his ego off.

This recounting may seem like workplace complaining, but research reveals that my experience is *the* experience for the majority of faculty.[1] It helps explain why most non-tenure part-time (NTPT) faculty express feeling trapped in a career that does not resemble what they signed up for.[2] In a survey I sent to NTPT faculty, an English instructor of four years said, "I used to be excited about my job, but I have become increasingly disillusioned and bitter about it." Similarly, an English instructor of seven years shared, "It was a great experience at the beginning which has slowly transformed into a very resentful and burnt-out attitude." An anthropology instructor of 15 years explained, "I have grown to dislike my workplace more and more over time." Some NTPT faculty argue that the time one spends in academia is synonymous with how disillusioned one becomes. "Slowly demoralizing" was how a writing instructor of 42 years described their career.

When queried if NTPT faculty would recommend a career in higher education to students, they responded in the negative: "No. I actively discourage it"; "Absolutely not—why waste time and money until you finally learn what's going on & become disillusioned?"; "No unless you recognize that you will be underpaid and underappreciated"; "NO. It is a long slog to get a PhD and even then [there is] the job scarcity and precariousness"; "Fuck no, "NO, NO!!"; "No. The future is even more contingency and I would not recommend this path to others"; and "HELL NO." Tenure and tenure-track (TT) faculty may have a similar experience, but without the precarity that defines the NTPT faculty.

This chapter utilizes surveys and existing research to examine the way neoliberalism has shaped the careers of faculty and its impact on learning and scholarship. Prior to the neoliberal era, faculty had established workplace agreements with campuses, such as tenure and academic freedom, which protected them in their scholarship and teaching and established faculty as a genuine profession. But the rise of neoliberal governance in higher education devalued the production of knowledge in favor of revenue generation. Instead of protecting scholarly inquiry, administrators sought to treat faculty as flexible labor whose primary function was to maximize enrollment and tuition. To accomplish this, institutions worked to dismantle the strong collective bargaining power that accompanied tenure and professional autonomy. They replaced secure, full-time faculty with contingent, low-paid instructors—the NTPT. This transition was the primary mechanism for weakening the profession, eroding both the practice and the purpose of academic freedom in the process.

Why Tenure Matters

Tenure in the United States emerged in the early twentieth century and was formalized with the American Association of University Professors' (AAUP) 1915 *Declaration of Principles on Academic*

Freedom and Academic Tenure.[3] Designed to protect scholars from arbitrary dismissal and political interference, tenure ensured that faculty could research, teach, and engage the public without fear of reprisal. By the 1940s, especially with the publication of the AAUP's 1940 *Statement of Principles on Academic Freedom and Tenure,* the system had become widely adopted, establishing a foundation of intellectual independence that defined U.S. higher education.[4]

At the core of tenure is academic freedom, a negotiated professional right that allows faculty to investigate controversial topics, question dominant ideologies, and express informed dissent in their scholarship and teaching.[5] The AAUP defines academic freedom as "freedom of a teacher or researcher in higher education to investigate and discuss the issues in his or her academic field, and to teach or publish findings without interference from political figures, boards of trustees, donors, or other entities. Academic freedom also protects the right of a faculty member to speak freely when participating in institutional governance, as well as to speak freely as a citizen."[6] Academic freedom serves the public good by ensuring that knowledge is produced through inquiry rather than ideology. It preserves the university as a space where ideas can be tested and debated, even when they prove inconvenient or unsettling, without jeopardizing one's career.

Tenure and academic freedom were never intended to shield ineffective or lazy employees, as critics often claim. Instead, they were established to ensure that scholars could pursue knowledge wherever it led, even when their findings threatened powerful interests. Researchers needed assurance they could reveal the link between smoking and cancer without fear that tobacco companies would pressure administrators to silence them; the same holds true for climate science in relation to fossil fuel interests, or for historians publishing uncomfortable truths about slavery or government complicity with fascism. Tenure does not prevent faculty from being fired; it simply prevents them from being fired for their viewpoints or for producing unpopular conclusions. Because the pursuit of knowledge is an inherently messy process, one that involves mistakes, false starts, and engagement with unsettled or even offensive ideas, academic freedom protects the experimentation necessary for eventual breakthroughs.[7]

These principles were tested dramatically in 1947 at the University of California, when faculty protested new loyalty oath requirements forcing them to swear that they had no ties to "subversive" organizations.[8] Many saw the oath as a direct attack on academic freedom and a betrayal of the protections promised by tenure. Dozens of faculty members refused to sign and were subsequently dismissed or resigned. Their collective action resulted in public condemnation and legal proceedings that deemed the oath unconstitutional. Although the protest from faculty took time, and some of the participants had to wait years before being reinstated, the 1947–1950 UC loyalty oath crisis remains a defining reminder of how fragile academic freedom can become and how effective collective action by faculty can be.[9]

Faculty Fragmented

As the 1947-1950 UC loyalty oath crisis demonstrated, labor solidarity amongst faculty can act as a form of pressure to extract concessions from a higher education institution. Thus, the power and influence of the professional managerial class (PMC) depend upon a divided faculty.

The PMC often uses the old divide-and-conquer tactics to weaken faculty solidarity. One of these tactics is merit pay, a system in which salary increases depend on individual performance. It is based on the capitalist assumption that competition with other faculty for merit pay will motivate faculty to improve their contributions to the campus.[10] Rather than negotiate better working conditions as a collective, as faculty did when combatting the 1947 loyalty oath, faculty compete against one another and negotiate merit pay individually.[11]

The most pervasive tactic the PMC used to divide faculty is the proliferation of NTPT faculty. Starting in the 1990s, budget cuts, many self-imposed by universities, were used as an excuse to replace tenure-track (TT) jobs with low-paid adjunct roles. In 1969, TT positions made up approximately 78.3 percent of faculty, while NTPT positions were about 21.7 percent.[12] Today, over two-thirds of faculty—or 68 percent—hold NTPT appointments, with less than 32 percent in TT positions.[13] Simultaneously, under the banner of efficiency, the PMC asserted that the diminished pool of TT faculty was no longer sufficient for meaningful participation in shared governance. Consequently, the faculty's traditional role in joint decision-making was curtailed, supplanted by bureaucratic management led primarily by administrators.[14] What was supposed to be a temporary fix became permanent.[15] The real goal wasn't just to temporarily survive budget cuts; it was to break faculty's collective power by making adjuncts the majority. This move effectively shattered the profession's unity and weakened its voice.

In higher education, faculty exist in two starkly different worlds. On one side are TT professors, 80 percent of whom earned their PhDs from the same elite 20 percent of doctoral-granting institutions.[16] Competitive salaries, job security, and benefits insulate them from the precarity that besets the other side, where adjuncts reside as NTPT faculty. For NTPT faculty, insecurity is the norm: low pay, minimal or no benefits, and little protection.[17] Their life is far from uniform. Some piece together contracts across multiple campuses, while others remain at a single institution on precarious terms. On average, adjuncts earn about $3,500 per class, for a total around $21,000 to $35,000 annually.[18] Only a few institutions offer meaningful benefits. One study found that 40 percent of NTPT faculty struggle to cover basic household costs, with 25 percent relying on public assistance.[19] Many survive by teaching more than a full-time load across campuses.

The Invisible Struggle of NTPT Faculty

"Well, I think you've got me beat this term, I'm only teaching twelve classes," my friend joked at the urinal. We've been friends for over a decade; he teaches on the East Coast, I'm on the West. Once a year, we meet at a conference, and when no one is around, such as in this bathroom, we compare workloads. It's our gallows humor, a way to cope. We've dubbed ourselves "road scholars" or "freeway fliers" because of the endless commutes that checker our careers. Swapping stories about students, administrators, and absurd situations with colleagues is how all of us pass the time.

Many TT faculty are unaware of this existence, because NTPT, out of a mix of shame and fear that it will be used against us, hide our experience. As a result, they often refer to us as "part-time" faculty, assuming we teach on the same campus as they do and maybe one other, on a "part-time" basis. Nothing could be further from the truth. Low pay and vanishing benefits force many NTPT faculty to piece together work across multiple campuses, carrying workloads that usually exceed 200 percent and can go as high as 400 percent. One anonymous instructor reported working 80-hour weeks across seven campuses for more than twenty years.[20] I can't count how many times a seasoned NTPT has leaned over and whispered, "How many classes are you teaching this term?" After I answer, they laugh, share their own crazy schedules from years past, then shrug: "I'm too old for that now. But you're young, you can handle it." It's a weary sort of encouragement coming from those who've lived through years of exploitation.

Life planning—whether it be for children, retirement, vacation, or a Zumba class—is impossible for NTPT faculty. Their schedule is just too unpredictable. Schedules are set months in advance at some campuses, only days before classes at others. Each campus maintains specific limits on the number of courses an NTPT faculty member may teach, with maximum allowable loads ranging from sixty-seven percent to a full-time appointment of one hundred percent—and in some cases, reaching as high as one hundred twenty-five percent.

When NTPT instructors are acclimating to a campus, it's common to waste precious minutes locating the classroom. Sometimes rooms change without notice, and they only find out by checking their roster moments before class begins. I learned this the hard way my first semester teaching: I showed up early to set up, only to realize I was in the wrong room.

Technology rarely makes things easier. Arriving early to class to test equipment is essential, because it often doesn't work. I've seen instructors rip cords and break cabinets out of frustration. One even busted open an electrical panel—technically vandalism—just to shut off a freezing AC unit. Logging into systems can be a nightmare, with two-factor authentication and mandatory password changes often locking faculty out minutes before class begins. Anxiety builds as NTPT faculty race across campuses, hoping everything, from traffic to parking to the room assignment and tech, cooperate so they can actually start teaching on time.

Parking is another daily headache: some campuses charge fees; others don't, but finding a spot close enough to avoid being late is always a race against time. If parking spots aren't available, adjuncts circle endlessly, losing valuable prep time. Once, I noticed a faculty member remove an "Employee of the Month" parking sign from a spot that was never used. For the rest of the time I taught on that campus, I followed his lead. I would remove the sign, park, make it to class with less than a minute to spare, then put the sign back when I left.

Everyone develops their own survival strategies. For me, I'd schedule the earliest class at the farthest campus to beat traffic, then work my way back toward home, stopping along the way at a campus or three to teach a course. Some days this meant driving for over an hour at dawn, rushing between campuses, barely finding time to eat or use the restroom. Forget those basics, and you risk showing up hungry or late, apologizing mid-class as your body betrays you.

Scheduling is only half the battle. If your class doesn't hit minimum enrollment before some arbitrary date set by the administration, it can be canceled. I learned this the hard way during my second term. In response, I changed my approach. I took as many classes as possible across as many campuses as possible so a cancellation wouldn't drop me below a livable wage. But it's not just the total number of enrollments that NTPT faculty have to gauge. If TT faculty, who get first choice of which classes they teach, have a class canceled due to low enrollment, they can bump NTPT faculty off the schedule and take their course. And on some campuses, senior NTPT faculty can bump junior ones. All this jockeying happens before the semester starts, when NTPT are not yet paid.

Even simple things like office space are hard to come by. Many adjuncts never get dedicated offices. If they do, it's often shared with several others, making it nearly impossible to have private conversations or prep in peace. Classroom access can be a nightmare, too. Some rooms unlock only when security arrives early in the morning, usually during the early teaching hours that tenured faculty are not interested in teaching. This results in NTPT faculty waiting around, hoping security shows up on time. One biology instructor waited nearly a whole semester to get keys for the lab where they taught twice a week in the morning. They had to rely on colleagues for access or call security each morning in order to do their job.

While I could share these struggles with other NTPT faculty, talking openly with TT faculty was rare. Class assignments often depend on subjective decisions unless contractually guaranteed, so many adjuncts keep their workloads secret, worried that revealing too much could be used against them. Whoever is in charge of scheduling—a department chair or dean or provost—may make small talk and ask, "Teaching anywhere else next term?" A naïve NTPT will answer honestly, only to have the person respond, "I'm worried you can't manage that load." Or, tenured faculty, shielded from these pressures, might ask, "Why do you work so much?"—not realizing many adjuncts must juggle multiple jobs just to survive.

This secrecy breeds isolation. NTPT faculty withdraw from tenured faculty and administrators, afraid to be honest about their lives. They report little interaction with tenured colleagues, describing relationships as "segregated," "distant," or "a kind of apartheid on campus." One writing instructor told me, "There's a real split between the handful of tenured instructors and the contingent faculty." Many reported having no meaningful connections at all. Interaction with administrators is even rarer. One NTPT faculty member said, "I never see them," while another admitted, "I avoid them and only talk to them as little as possible to keep some autonomy."

It works both ways. I was a representative on a union which, according to a colleague, once bargained to force university managers to meet with NTPT faculty once a year upon hiring, and the university refused to negotiate that into the contract. The university did not want its managers to meet their own employees. As a result of decisions like this, loneliness becomes yet another burden for NTPT faculty in an already tough job. Segregation from colleagues deepens the divide among faculty, which makes building solidarity and collaborating across campus to improve education much more difficult.

The Galactic Divide

TT and NTPT faculty live in completely different worlds, fighting for different things, and that makes it nearly impossible to come together as a collective force against university management. At many schools, NTPT faculty have had to form their own unions and build their rights from scratch, while tenured faculty have been accruing protection and influence since the early to mid-20th century. The very nature of NTPT faculty work, with instructors coming and going and only present on campus when teaching, makes building strong collective faculty power a huge challenge. Without steady presence and consistent connections, organizing is an uphill battle.

Life as NTPT faculty requires navigating a complex social landscape with tenured colleagues. Some are allies, some are indifferent, and some wield their tenure as a subtle form of power. Relationships vary widely, from supportive to downright hostile, and the divide between tenured and non-tenured faculty often reflects deeper issues of entitlement and elitism. An NTPT instructor of twelve years captured the spectrum perfectly: "Some pity us, others are contemptuous of us, and some are our de facto employers."

Other TT colleagues seem completely oblivious to NTPT faculty's day-to-day struggles. An NTPT who taught for forty-two years explained it as a process by which tenured faculty become "willingly oblivious and deluded into thinking they are special or lucky." While some NTPT faculty acknowledged that certain TT faculty worked hard to earn their tenure, they claimed that many are "entitled slackers." An NTPT instructor of fourteen years put it bluntly: "TT faculty are a mixture of hard workers and others who got the job based on who they know, not what they know. The first [hard workers] are great to work with; however, the latter [are] often entitled and not very interested in sharing the load." An NTPT English instructor of four years added: "I respect many of the tenure-track faculty in my department. Of course, there are some 'villains' who seem to be bad people, and there are quite a few octogenarians who make $175k+/year while making a minimal effort to teach and relying on ancient mimeographed notes from the 1970s instead of trying to adapt their teaching to the evolving world."

NTPT faculty also note how disrespected they feel by many TT colleagues. They described TT faculty as frequently acting "rather arrogant" and treating NTPT faculty like a "gnat or even a mosquito." They often see themselves as "too good for adjuncts," whom they view as "not as smart." One participant shared a telling story about an email: "One tenured faculty wrote an aggressively disrespectful email that was both mocking and sarcastic about adjunct parity, claiming that increasing parity would rob full timers of fair wages." Another NTPT faculty member summarized the disrespect by saying, "Tenure track [faculty], at times, come off as an elite who have little reason to work with second-class scholars."

Not all tenured faculty are hostile toward NTPTs the way Napoleon is. Many former NTPTs who earned tenure, and even some department chairs, understand the critical role adjuncts play and are genuinely supportive. They would treat me like part of the team, and I felt valued. They recognized the importance of my scholarship and pedagogy. Some NTPT faculty noted similar experiences. An NTPT composition instructor of fifteen years told me, "I have some tenured faculty who openly advocate for us and have done so for me. They have led me to professional opportunities and training. That's a give or take." An NTPT anatomy and physiology instructor of three years added, "Some tenure-track faculty see the regular non-tenure-track faculty as working their way up to their position and are very helpful and want to do everything they can to help the kind of freshman faculty work their way through the system."

Echoing my own experience, NTPT faculty noted that the tenured faculty showing the most empathy tend to be those who started out as NTPT instructors themselves. An NTPT history instructor explained: "The tenured faculty I have worked with at the community college level are helpful because they started as adjunct instructors." In fact, I've had numerous department chairs and provosts, some of whom had once been NTPT faculty, and they were amazingly supportive. One told me that they have a form of "survivor's guilt" about making it into a TT faculty position. This is not too surprising, as solidarity generally comes easily from a shared experience such as being an NTPT faculty. That is precisely what the adjunctification of higher education seeks to avoid.

Power Plays and Precarity

The relationship between management and faculty is similarly strained. Management exists to enforce policies handed down from the executive level. Some faculty, especially those hoping to move into administrative roles, try to cultivate good relationships with them. Older faculty who remember a time before the PMC's dominance in higher education often ignore managers altogether, relying on tenure for protection. For NTPT faculty, the relationship is more fraught. Management enforces burdensome policies that drain time and energy from teaching and scholarship, yet it also serves as a referee in conflicts between NTPT faculty and tenure-track faculty, or between NTPT instructors and students.

The most "effective" managers accept process as purpose. They suppress independent thought and simply follow the procedures handed down from higher up the bureaucratic ladder. An NTPT English instructor summed it up bluntly, "Managers tend to be the kind of people who would be miserable in any normal office job, but somehow, they thrive in campus bureaucracy. Sure, some do important work, but most are just leeches, making campus culture as bland, corporate, and soulless as any office cubicle farm. They're paper pushers, pure and simple."

There is a sense among faculty that managers are aloof to the impact their behaviors have on NTPT faculty. For example, a private college needed a last-minute replacement for a teacher who came down with an illness midsemester. I volunteered. The dean set a meeting for 3 p.m. At 3 p.m., the dean was still away from her office. At 3:30, I emailed asking what was going on. The reply? "I saw adding this course to your load would put you over the maximum assignment of 100 percent." Rather than tell me directly, she just moved on to the next NTPT faculty member and ignored our meeting without even the courtesy of a cancellation notice. It is behavior such as this that leads people like one NTPT art instructor to conclude that managers are "out of touch with the daily struggles of low pay and job insecurity," and a social work instructor to add, "They don't understand that schedule changes don't work when you have multiple jobs." Other faculty describe administrators as "condescending," "rude," and "dismissive." Still others use words like "ruthless," "exploitative," and "aloof" to describe their bosses.

I have seen managers leverage their power and NTPT precarity for labor exploitation. For instance, while contracts say faculty shouldn't have to exceed certain class sizes, administrators send emails like, "It would really help if you could add a few more students," or "Could you do us a favor and squeeze in two more?" Many NTPT faculty are too afraid to say no, as it may lead to them being replaced by one who will say yes.

I've met some amazing administrators, including friends like the dean who helped me land part-time work with student services or the provosts who fought to get my courses approved and expanded my schedule. It's not all negative. Some adjuncts recognize that administrators are often just people trapped in a broken system. "When I think about them in the abstract, I hold them in contempt," one said, "but when I meet them, I realize they're mostly normal people trying to get by." Others point out that administrators answer to higher-ups and rules faculty never see, which means what's "best" for programs isn't always clear-cut. Some even reported good relationships: "I love the admin people," one said, and another added, "I have great rapport with my administrators." Indeed, many administrators I know who once were faculty members often laugh cynically as they describe the bureaucratic requirements they must enforce. They share how soul-crushing administrative work can be, explaining that it aligns with David Graeber's research on "bullshit jobs," positions people recognize as meaningless but feel compelled to do in order to make a living.[21]

De-Professionalizing the Profession

The division among faculty and the power of the PMC in higher education results in the deprofessionalization of higher education faculty. Faculty have long been considered professionals because they have specialized training and expertise, uphold high ethical standards, provide competent paid service, demonstrate responsibility, continuous learning, and strong conduct. As professionals, the issuers of the 1940 AAUP statement did recommend a probationary period of no more than seven years for new full-time faculty, but the intent was to force institutions to either grant a full-time tenured position or remove faculty from the institution.[22] In the mid-20th century, when TT jobs dominated the profession, tenure review and decisions were primarily under the authority of the administration, which included the boards of trustees, presidents, and senior academic administrators, rather than faculty.

In the neoliberal era, faculty became the primary evaluators of their peers' competence.[23] Because most often faculty are divided into NTPT and TT, these evaluation systems raise serious concerns on several fronts. The evaluations themselves do not serve to improve the scholarship faculty produce or their teaching. Indeed, research shows that evaluations are largely subjective.[24] This is due in part to a lack of clear guidelines and criteria for what evaluators are evaluating.[25]

In addition to the unclear guidelines, the data used in evaluation is subjective. Evaluations often rely on anonymous student feedback, which research reveals frequently reflects implicit bias more than actual teaching effectiveness. Female faculty, faculty of color, and younger instructors are disproportionately penalized as compared to their older white, male colleagues for similar behaviors.[26] When I raised this issue on social media, women faculty shared evaluations in which students had referred to them as "b**ch," and one female faculty member said that in an evaluation a student wrote, "she looked like she needed to be raped."

Even when student evaluations are objective, they reveal very little in terms of how to improve the classroom. Students are given a numerical rating on a scale of 1 to 5, with prompts such as, "My instructor responds to my communications in a timely fashion, do you agree or disagree?" They also include open-ended questions like, "What was the most valuable part of this course?" or "What was the most challenging part of this course?" allowing students to provide qualitative feedback. Some say, "I honestly do not have a suggestion." Some make complaints about things we cannot change, "I wish the class was at a better time?" I do not make the schedule. Others offer complaints that are out of step with classroom reality. One student once said, "I think there is too much reading." How much is enough? By what metric? Which student's expertise counts? Furthermore, since they are anonymous, we do not know who the student is. A student who showed up to class and knew the material ought to carry more weight than someone who never showed up or did the work.

These student-led evaluations have turned higher education into Yelp University, where much like on the popular Yelp review site, people with no direct teaching experience judge and rate educators. After all, what is the value in collecting data about effective teaching from students who have never taught? Yes, they possess different skills, knowledge, and positionality than an instructor, but what does that have to do with their understanding of teaching? This isn't personal. I also reject the mad rush to evaluate everyone everywhere. Why do I evaluate my doctor, my mechanic, or my barista? They know their jobs. I do not know how to do their job. Who am I to comment on it? Students, despite limited context or expertise, are empowered to judge faculty performance. It is a mechanism for de-professionalizing the profession by having non-professionals judge professional performance.

The fact that evaluations are useless does not mean that they are not a mechanism of control in higher education. The evaluation also furthers the divide among faculty. TT colleagues evaluate each other, treat the process as routine, and give uniformly positive reviews to avoid conflict. Research shows that institutional hierarchies and implicit bias can shape peer evaluations.[27] Given the power that TT faculty possess to evaluate and schedule NTPT faculty, the evaluation is a subjective opportunity to keep a colleague they like or remove one they dislike, regardless of performance. This is not hypothetical. I know of a department that ousted a faculty member over a single complaint claiming they brought a puppy to class. In another case, tenured faculty cherry-picked only negative comments from students to push an NTPT instructor onto probation. In yet another incident, a tenured professor fabricated a student complaint outright to remove an NTPT colleague from the department.

Collective bargaining units often fail to protect NTPT from predatory evaluations because they represent both sides of the conflict. In one case, a union where I served on declined to file a grievance on behalf of an NTPT faculty member out of fear it would expose misconduct by a tenured faculty member.

Scholarship in Crisis: When Efficiency Undermines Innovation

Just as faculty members struggle to uphold effective teaching under the neoliberal assault, they face similar challenges in maintaining effective scholarship. Scholarship is supposed to be the defining output of higher education. Universities are meant to be sites of knowledge production, where scholars labor to create new ideas, test hypotheses, and expand human understanding. Students who are serious about learning, or about joining this intellectual tradition, enroll in college to be part of that process.

A 2020 study by Nicholas Bloom, Charles I. Jones, John Van Reenen, and Michael Webb, economists at Stanford and MIT, titled "Are Ideas Getting Harder to Find?" concluded that despite more scientists, more papers, and more experiments, progress in fields from medicine to agriculture is slowing. For example, they observe that in heart-disease research, publications and clinical trials have soared, yet the extension of human life per unit of effort has diminished. In other words, scientific discovery is no longer keeping pace with the inputs we pour into it.

This slowdown is not a mystery; it is the result of what Benjamin Jones calls the "burden of knowledge."[28] As a field matures, the low-hanging fruit – the easy breakthroughs –have already been picked. Achieving each new advance requires more researchers, more money, and greater depth of expertise. Ezra Klein and Derek Thompson note in *Abundance* that discovering something truly novel is no longer a solo pursuit, like Mendel with his pea plants or the early elemental discoveries; it requires coordinated teams, years of work, and complex infrastructure.[29] Genome-wide studies of schizophrenia, CRISPR gene-editing, and PCR-based diagnostics which act like a molecular photocopier, all illustrate that today's breakthroughs are built on decades of incremental knowledge and painstaking effort. The implication is clear: if we want to maintain the same level of innovation, we need more people and more resources, not less.

Yet neoliberal policies have done the opposite. Budget cuts, bureaucratic expansion, and a fixation on "efficiency" have constrained the very resources that knowledge-intensive work requires. Agencies like the NIH, once the engines of bold discovery, now emphasize grant-writing, compliance paperwork, and low-risk projects over high-reward research.[30] Young scientists—the primary engines of groundbreaking innovation—are frequently marginalized, forced to squander their peak years of potential discovery and scientific inquiry on drafting grant proposals for distant bureaucrats.

The corporate logic of neoliberalism sees too much of scholarship as inefficient and wasteful, when in fact, it produces substantive research. Higher education takes on the financial and intellectual risks of trial and error: we test ideas, discard the ones that fail, and refine those that show promise. Even negative results are valuable, because they help us discover what doesn't work, as well as what might.[31] Yet, in the neoliberal era, when something does succeed, commercial entities swoop in to capitalize on it, taking the profits and the credit, while accusing public education of being bloated, wasteful, or inefficient. Indeed, foundational technologies like semiconductors, the internet, GPS, and touchscreen interfaces all originated from publicly funded research before being privatized and commercialized.[32]

The combined effect of these neoliberal policies and structural bottlenecks is a decline in the quality of scholarship. We see the consequences in medicine, as cancer research progresses unevenly despite decades of investment, and life-saving drugs are often incremental rather than revolutionary.[33] The very structure of the U.S. research system, shaped by policy choices and bureaucratic priorities, is now constraining innovation at precisely the moment when scientific fields demand greater collaboration, deeper talent, and bolder ambition. The lesson is stark: treating scholarship like a line-item to be streamlined or cut undermines the conditions for genuine discovery, proving that neoliberal governance comes at a profound cost to the advancement of knowledge.

In addition, neoliberal policies serve to shrink the number of people who can realistically engage in scholarship. Graduate degrees, which once served as a ticket to well-paid, secure tenure-track positions, have increasingly become pathways to exploited adjunct labor. A generation or two ago, young scholars could pursue areas of genuine interest, supported by funded programs and graduate student research. Today, most new PhDs face a landscape in which tenure-track jobs are vanishing, and the majority of faculty positions are NTPT thus do not require or reward publishing. A media studies instructor explained coming to that realization, "when my application for Institutional Review Board (IRB) approval was rejected because 'lecturers are unable to be principal investigators' for their own projects." The old adage 'publish or perish' is fading—not because publishing has lost its importance, but because the majority of PhDs who remain in academia are relegated to lecturer roles that systematically deny them the opportunity to lead research; this is the inevitable consequence of a deeply entrenched, elitist system.

Still, administrators cannot fully purge scholarship. Parents and students continue to expect some visible presence of scholars as proof that their tuition is paying for a "real" education. As a result, universities keep a handful of scholars on staff, not because their research is valued but because their existence is useful marketing. Scholarship has been reduced to a prop in the university's sales pitch: evidence of "prestige" for brochures and campus tours, while in reality the institution treats the work of scholarship as disposable, inconvenient, and even threatening to its bottom line.

Conclusion

The vision of higher education that once inspired future academics now feels like a distant relic of another age. In reality, anyone entering the profession would be wiser to prepare for maneuvering a battlefield than for thoughtful exchanges with scholars. Much of their time will be consumed by bureaucratic procedures that do little to enhance teaching or research. They will be evaluated by managers and students who may never have taught a class, all while watching their backs to ensure a colleague does not use some procedural mechanism to undermine their career.

It wasn't always this way. Faculty fought hard to secure protections like tenure and academic freedom, establishing themselves in a true profession dedicated to the pursuit of knowledge. But neoliberal governance reshaped higher education into a revenue-driven exploitation machine that divides faculty and consolidates power among the PMC. Instead of safeguarding inquiry, administrators reduced faculty to flexible labor focused primarily on maximizing enrollment and tuition. Collective bargaining power was dismantled as a result. What about the students? The ones who pay huge amounts of tuition to take courses from exhausted faculty who would not recommend the profession to the people they are teaching. They are the subject of the next chapter.

3

Students as Customers and Products

As I was wrapping up my doctoral program in Education, I realized I had completed all the requirements to graduate an entire semester early. I had followed the advice of friends and colleagues who warned me that graduate school was not a place to linger. Throughout my time in academia, I had seen and heard of many students who languished in graduate school for years. Some faced legitimate hardships; others clung to unrealistic expectations about their dissertations. Some stayed six to seven years beyond the graduation date only to abandon the program without a degree.

In academia, having your published work cited is a badge of honor that opens doors for career advancement. Tenure-track jobs depend on your publication record, hence the age-old saying: *publish or perish*. To determine "quality" studies, the neoliberal era saw a rising use of impact factors, numerical metrics used to signal how frequently a study or journal was cited. The more cited, the more competitive. To prevent graduate students from getting stuck in perpetual dissertation mode, seasoned faculty often repeat another mantra: *The best dissertation is a completed dissertation.* The point is to remind students that the dissertation is evidence of their academic abilities, not the pinnacle of their career. The longer you spend on it, the more you pay, whether in tuition, lost earnings, or both.

I heeded these warnings from colleagues, I expediently chose my research topic and began work on what became my dissertation in my first term. The program was well organized and allowed me to focus much of my coursework on my dissertation. The summer before my final year of graduate school, I completed a polished draft that I was ready to defend. This required presenting my dissertation to a panel of faculty and students who would approve (or disprove, in the unfortunate event) of the work, making me eligible to receive the degree. Curious whether I could graduate early, I consulted someone who directed a similar program within our university system. He confirmed that I should be eligible to finish a semester ahead of schedule.

I mentioned this in casual conversation to the director of my doctoral program; we'll call her Hillary. I liked Hillary on a personal level. She was approachable, humorous, and very intelligent. I admired her ability to run a classroom that was both rigorous and inviting. However, like nearly everyone else in the program, students and faculty alike, with the exception of my dissertation chair, she was a neoliberal: someone who believed that corporate models in education could deliver social justice. Because my own work critically examined how neoliberalism shaped my real passion, media literacy, I would tread lightly when discussing anything that might conflict with the dominant ideology.

Hillary's normally cheerful demeanor shifted, almost instantly, to anger and derision when I brought up graduating early. She insisted that the faculty member I had consulted didn't know what he was talking about. On one level, she was correct, but not for the reasons I had assumed.

Technically, the regulations governing our program allowed students to graduate early if they had completed their coursework. But the faculty who designed my program had intentionally required a course offered only in the spring, effectively forcing all students to remain for the full duration and pay the full tuition. This was corporatism disguised as pedagogy. The program's design was justified because it is ensured fiscal viability, but at the cost of tuition and time from students. The requirement served financial interests, not educational ones.

I stayed, and I paid. This was academic capitalism in action, a phenomenon Sheila Slaughter and Larry Leslie describe as universities and faculty behaving like entrepreneurial agents, prioritizing revenue generation over knowledge-driven missions.[1] In the neoliberal logic of the program's designers, ensuring tuition in exchange for education reflected the monetization of what Pierre Bourdieu called *academic capital*: the value derived from education and scholarly achievement.[2]

Within an academic capitalist framework, students are customers. The goal of colleges and universities is to persuade students to spend their capital in exchange for the goods and services associated with education. For many students, the capital is borrowed through massive student loans that will burden them for decades. Students, like all other customers, are persuaded to take out loans through marketing: glossy mailers, brochures, commercials, social media posts, videos, and websites. Each year, my media literacy students and I analyze these advertisements, and what stands out is how rarely scholars, academics, or classrooms appear in them. Instead, schools sell an airbrushed fantasy they describe as a "transformative college experience."

To deliver on this "experience," institutions weaponize the bloated bureaucracy to ensure that the student's "journey" is comprised of faculty who give passing grades and only challenge students to the extent that they are comfortable. Discouraged dropouts are bad for business, since they negatively affect college rankings that students and parents use to determine whether a school is worth the cost. Because parents often foot the bill and expect a return on their investment, universities need scholars they can market as "leaders in their fields." This is the primary reason institutions begrudgingly keep a small number of tenure-track faculty around, so parents feel reassured that their child is receiving a *legitimate* education.

Academic capitalism's degradation of students to customers undermines education in two critical ways. First, higher education is supposed to be a place of growth and learning. Students must confront the reality that they will not excel at everything immediately: that is the purpose of education. Second, the production of knowledge, and the scholars who create it, should be central to higher education, not peripheral to a manufactured "experience" where students play volleyball while listening to whatever corporate-approved artist the campus claims is profound.

The vision of growth and learning collapses when administrators routinely override the expertise of scholars and teachers, empowering students to act as the "experts" who evaluate their instructors and police them through classroom bias reporting systems. The problem is compounded by initiatives like "cost-free textbooks," which, within a capitalist society where price signals value, suggest to students that scholarship has none. Predictably, students start to see scholars as people who couldn't make it in the "real world," trapped in the academic bubble producing "boring" studies that "no one reads." In this narrative, scholars become pedantic obstacles standing between students and the carefree "college experience" they were promised.

This mindset, reinforced by marketing, administrative language, and grade inflation, leads students and parents to adopt a marketplace logic: *the customer is always right.* The result is a familiar refrain: "I paid my tuition, so where's my passing grade?" Faculty become service workers. Administrative messaging frequently utilizes service-oriented language that frames the student-teacher relationship as a commercial transaction. "The customer has ordered an 'A'!" This commodification is reinforced by the implementation of Customer Management Systems (CMS), which analyze student data. CMS refers to students as customers and prioritizes market analytics over sound pedagogy.

Taken together, these trends—rising tuition, corporate influence in the classroom, and the commodification of students and knowledge—paint a clear picture: higher education has transformed into a marketplace first and a site of learning second. Students are no longer simply learners; they are customers, data points, and sometimes products to be mined and marketed. Administrators prioritize branding, retention, and revenue over rigorous education, while corporations see campuses as laboratories for profit-driven experimentation.

A Brief History of College Costs

Shortly before the 2011 Occupy Wall Street movement began—later to be crushed by neoliberal governments across the country –I was in graduate school for my Master of Arts Program. During that time, I helped organize a rally to protest tuition hikes. By the time I entered my master's program, I was well aware tuition was high. I had been accepted to a PhD program on the East Coast that same year, and when I called to inquire about costs, I remember asking, "Do you think tuition will go up next year, when I plan to attend?" The kind voice on the other end laughed and replied, "I've been here since 1995, and it's gone up every year I've been here."

Our rally was pretty lame at first. We set up near a grassy area, and only a handful of people showed up. So, we decided to wander around campus to see if others might join us. Eventually, we stumbled upon a large group of students gathered outside the library, not in the library. One of them jokingly shouted, "Bring your rally here!" We looked at each other, shrugged, and went back to grab our table. As we carried it across campus, something shifted. The energy of a few caught the attention of many. Students began joining us as we walked. By the time we reached the library, we suddenly had a real crowd.

The student newspaper arrived almost immediately, snapping photos and jotting down notes. I remember the moment clearly because it was the first time I ever spoke at a rally, and the first time I ever held a megaphone. I had always hoped to avoid becoming the kind of leader who delivered fiery speeches. Something about the art of impassioned persuasion made me uneasy; I was wary of anything that resembled demagoguery. But a friend introduced me anyway, knowing I didn't want to speak, and as he handed me the megaphone he whispered, "Sorry, brother, I had to do it."

He was an articulate, intelligent, and driven Mexican American student who would go on to have great success in the Democratic Party. I gave my speech, though I can't remember a word of what I said, and walked away thinking it was terrible. Yet, a handful of students came up afterward, patted me on the back, and thanked me for speaking. I thought they were just being nice, but it sure was a confidence boost, and I thanked my buddy for forcing me to get out of my comfort zone.

I think the rally—please allow me to call this thirty-minute burst of campus noise a "rally"—resonated because so many students felt powerless under an administration more concerned with balancing budgets than promoting learning. The fact that five people with twenty minutes of planning could draw the attention of students and the school newspaper said everything. A shared sense of indignation ran through campus, but so did a deep sense of inequity: students were overwhelmed by loans that would follow them well into adulthood, while faculty struggled to uphold academic standards despite ballooning class sizes and constant administrative pressure.

That tension, between the ideals of education and the realities of the marketplace, shapes how I interact with students today. And students are still feeling the burden. Despite our small rally and the far more serious efforts of countless activists, tuition continues to rise without end.

Was There Ever a "Golden Age"?

When people complain about tuition hikes, they often romanticize a supposed golden age of affordable, accessible higher education in the decades after World War II. But historian Elizabeth Tandy Shermer argues that this period was not golden at all, only gilded. Shermer contends that while the 1950s and 1960s saw rapid growth in colleges, rising federal aid, and the expansion of tenure-track jobs, these gains were uneven and deeply exclusionary. The benefits of that era were largely reserved for white men.[3]

Shermer's work is well researched, but the argument she makes has been distorted by neoliberals. They contend that anyone seeking to return to such a funding model is inherently trying to erase the gains made by historically marginalized communities, rather than proposing an agenda in which that funding model exists while fully including those communities. Their argument goes like this: because the postwar system was sexist, racist, and homophobic, advocating for robust public investment in higher education is simply nostalgia for a discriminatory past. This narrative conveniently ignores another possibility, one that is both achievable and historically grounded: a tuition-free system with plentiful tenure-track jobs and an inclusive student body. Achieving it would require substantial public spending, which in turn means taxing the wealthy and empowering government—two neoliberal taboos. So instead, reformers are dismissed as people longing for a racist and sexist era, rather than people envisioning a more equitable future.

Nonetheless, there *was* a time in U.S. history when federal programs, imperfect and exclusionary by today's standards, did significantly expand access. The Servicemen's Readjustment Act of 1944, commonly known as the GI Bill, provided returning World War II veterans with financial benefits such as tuition assistance and low-cost mortgages, enabling millions to attend college who otherwise could not afford it.[4] The Higher Education Act of 1965 increased federal funding for colleges and created financial aid programs such as Pell Grants, which are a form of no-repayment need-based financial aid provided by the U.S. government to help undergraduate students pay for college, and student loans, making higher education more accessible to a wider population.[5] Together, these laws opened the doors to millions of students, significantly expanding access to college even as they reinforced existing racial and economic inequalities. Crucially, the aid they offered came primarily in the form of loans and competitive grants, not direct public funding designed to keep tuition low.

Tuition Keeps Climbing

With government-guaranteed loans, corporations—focused on maximizing profits—pressured higher education institutions to increase student loan borrowing as a way to generate more revenue. In the college years between 1999–2000 and 2019–2020, tuition at public four-year institutions soared by 84 percent, far outpacing the 15.7 percent growth in median household income during the same period.[6] While room and board costs also increased, they did so at a slower rate. By 2020, tuition and fees at public colleges consumed over 35 percent of median household income, up from 18 percent just two decades earlier.[7] The situation is even worse at private institutions, where tuition reached 137 percent of median income.[8] This rapid inflation has priced many families out of higher education entirely, or left students burdened with crushing debt.

Several structural forces rooted in the neoliberal reshaping of higher education drive these increases. Administrative bloat has ballooned, with more staff hired to manage everything from compliance to marketing.[9] Universities have invested heavily in expensive new buildings, athletic facilities, and technology upgrades, often more as branding tools than as educational necessities. Meanwhile, healthcare and benefit costs for faculty and staff have risen sharply. Public universities, in particular, have been squeezed by steep state funding cuts, especially after the 2008 Great

Recession. As state subsidies declined from covering about 77 percent of public college revenue in the late 1980s to mostly under half since 2013, tuition was pushed upward to fill the financial gap.[10] In fact, 32 states spent less on higher education in 2020 than they did in 2008.[11]

To attract and retain students in an increasingly competitive market, colleges have expanded student services, including career centers, lazy rivers, climbing walls, luxury dorms, high-end dining, upgraded facilities, and tech perks. Spending on these amenities jumped dramatically in just a decade, reinforcing what many describe as an "amenities arms race," in which universities compete to offer more while shifting the cost burden onto families.[12] Unlike many developed countries, the U.S. lacks any regulatory mechanism to cap or subsidize tuition, leaving pricing to what the market can bear. Out-of-state and international students, who often pay two to three times more, provide cross-subsidies that further inflate tuition figures.[13]

Beyond administrative costs, two primary economic theories explain the persistent rise in tuition.[14] First is Baumol's cost disease, which suggests that costs rise in service sectors that experience low productivity growth, like education and healthcare. Because teaching remains a labor-intensive process that cannot be automated the way manufacturing can, productivity stays flat; however, institutions must still raise wages to prevent faculty from leaving for high-productivity industries. Second, the supply of higher education is inelastic, meaning colleges cannot easily expand facilities or enrollment to meet surges in demand. When the public is unwilling to fund the expansion of academic institutions, tuition naturally escalates to bridge the gap.

While federal student aid aims to provide relief, it often incentivizes institutions to raise tuition to capture those funds. Researchers suggest that because students have easy access to loans, colleges compete for enrollment by investing heavily in the "student experience." This manifests in lavish amenities such as concert halls, high-end dormitories, and luxury fitness centers. Ultimately, student loans may inadvertently fuel the very economic dynamics that drive tuition upward. This market-driven focus has contributed to a nearly 300 percent inflation-adjusted increase in public tuition and fees since 1963, with private institutions following a similar trajectory.[15]

Marketing an "Experience"

I'm always amused by college websites showing smiling students lounging on the grass, frisbee in hand, looking fresh and rested, as though campus life is one long yoga retreat. In reality, the students I see are often exhausted, disengaged, and scrolling through TikTok during lectures. Don't get me wrong, there are plenty of brilliant students who demonstrate deep critical thinking skills and thoughtful analysis. They arrive early to class, ask thoughtful questions, and often share ideas from outside the classroom that connect to our discussions. Having taught at nearly every type of institution and guest-lectured widely, I find that these engaged students are few and far between. Prior to the neoliberal era, this was not the case. Research reveals that in the 1960s and 1970s, an overwhelming majority of students at UCLA (over 80 percent) cited developing a meaningful philosophy of life as an "essential" or "very important" goal of their college education. By the 2010s up through today, that applied to less than half, as most students (over 80 percent) cite becoming financially very well-off in post college careers as their top goal.[16]

As the critical education scholar Henry Giroux argues, this is no accident. Neoliberal ideology has transformed higher education into a marketplace that commodifies learning, undermines democratic values, and recasts students as consumers and professors as disposable labor.[17] In this logic, administrators don't nurture intellectual growth. They package and sell an experience through glossy brochures, Instagrammable dorms, and promises of networking. Faculty, meanwhile, are expected to keep students engaged through entertaining pedagogy and, more important, keep them enrolled by ensuring they don't fail out. In other words: don't challenge students too much; they might take their tuition elsewhere.

Starting in the 1980s, this market logic of higher education was communicated to the public through ranking systems, which rely on subjective data to determine what is the "best" institution, in publications such as the *U.S. News & World Report*. These rankings quickly became central to how students choose colleges and how institutions market themselves.[18] Critics argue that these rankings reward wealth and exclusivity over educational quality.[19] Indeed, factors such as how many students are denied, alumni donations, and endowment size are treated as more valuable than meaningful outcomes like graduation rates for first-generation students.[20] The paradox is that while many universities grumble about rankings, nearly all continue to provide data and promote their placement if it's favorable.[21] The result is a self-reinforcing cycle in which rankings shape institutional priorities, which then shape what gets marketed to prospective students: return on investment, prestige, and "value." Genuine learning outcomes often feel like an afterthought.

If the 1980s and 1990s were about learning to play the rankings game, the 2000s brought calls for universities to adopt full-scale marketing strategies. By the 1990s, institutions facing financial strain and enrollment declines needed better ways to "sell" themselves to students and donors.[22] In the corporate mindset, marketing was no longer a dirty word; it was survival. As a result, colleges must implement "integrated strategic marketing" to thrive.[23] This means not just flashy ads or mailers, but enterprise-wide coordination: market research, differentiated branding, storytelling consistent with institutional values, and digital outreach. The vice president for marketing and communication at Stony Brook University, Teresa Flannery, argues that when done right, marketing can build long-term loyalty among students, alumni, donors, and partners – essentially a holistic customer relations model for higher ed.[24] This enables the institutions to continue to pursue patents, partnerships, and entrepreneurial ventures, reframing higher education not just as places of learning but as engines of innovation and growth.[25]

By prioritizing market-driven logic, modern universities have traded their role as spaces for critical inquiry for a consumer-oriented model that stifles intellectual freedom. University of Virginia professor and author Mark Edmundson argues that a university modeled after a marketplace inherently lacks the neutral, non-commercial environment students need to critique the market values they were raised to embrace.[26] Edmundson contends that this market influence fosters a corporate-leaning "frat-boy" culture that often dictates the social climate on campus.[27] In his 2018 work, *The Heart of the Humanities: Reading, Writing, Teaching*, he suggests that the chase for "consumer bliss" is actually a deceptive form of overstimulated bondage to the market rather than true liberty.[28] Edmundson points out that the market-driven logic currently embedded in higher education conditions students to achieve a hollow, self-policing existence as consumers, rather than encouraging them to reject, or at least approach with deep skepticism, the consumer society.

The Customer Is Always Right

A colleague once shared a story about a biology student who had failed the class with another instructor the previous term. When asked what they planned to do differently to avoid failing again, the student simply replied, "Nothing. I had a bad professor." This blunt response exemplifies a growing trend born from the corporatization of education: some students acting like customers feel entitled to the products they paid for, a passing grade and a degree. If those aren't delivered, the fault lies with the institution and its employees, because, after all, in customer service the customer is always right. Scholars have noted that the corporatization of higher education has created a weaker bond between faculty and students, as it is no longer mentor and mentee, but employee and customer.[29]

Higher education is not merely another consumer product. To truly learn, students must be challenged, allowed to fail, and encouraged to grow through intellectual discomfort; education is not always a comfortable process, nor should it be. However, when universities treat students as customers, the pedagogical dynamic shifts toward appeasement. It is now common for students to bypass faculty and appeal directly to department chairs or deans. Fearing litigation or bad PR, administrators often pressure faculty to provide passing grades regardless of a student's effort or mastery.

A recent incident at my institution illustrates this systemic rot. A student emailed the entire department and the President's office, claiming a professor had "wrongly" accused them of using so-called artificial intelligence (AI) on an assignment. Standard institutional protocol requires a student to first raise concerns with the instructor, then the Department Chair, then the Divisional Dean, and finally the Dean of Instruction before ever reaching the President. This student bypassed every safeguard and went straight to the top.

Worse yet, although faculty contracts explicitly forbid administrators from intervening before these steps are exhausted, the deans and the President intervened anyway. By entertaining the complaint and demanding the instructor provide "further information," they broke protocol and forced the faculty member into hours of unauthorized labor. Ultimately, the student inadvertently admitted that their "frustration" with the instructor had led them to use AI on other assignments—effectively proving the instructor's initial suspicion correct. The student was simply testing whether the administration would prioritize customer satisfaction over academic integrity.

A similar surrender occurred at the University of Oklahoma, where a professor made national headlines after failing a student who cited the Bible on an assignment where it was explicitly listed as an inappropriate source. Despite the student's failure to follow clear directions, the university—fearing accusations of religious persecution—placed the professor on leave.[30] In the consumer-driven university, the "crime" of a student failing to follow instructions is secondary to the administration's fear of a negative news cycle.

The Illusion of Excellence

With students conditioned to prioritize passing over genuine intellectual engagement, and faculty either inhibited by fear of losing their employment status or too jaded to resist battles with students, it is no wonder that grade inflation has become such a persistent challenge in higher education.[31] The corporate model of neoliberal education fundamentally incentivizes grade inflation through several institutional mechanisms. First, students are conditioned to expect courses to conform to their preferences rather than challenge them to grow; this is actively reinforced by institutional rhetoric such as "student centered classrooms" or we are here to *serve* our students, and practices such as anonymous student evaluations, mandated accommodations, bias reporting systems, and low-cost textbook initiatives. Concurrently, faculty, eager to boost enrollments, minimize the time wasted on complaints from students who prioritize passing, and to protect their employment, often resort to grade inflation. In a system designed to privilege measurable success over intellectual growth, inflated grades are not an aberration; they are the predictable outcome of the market-oriented university.

Indeed, grade inflation has become nothing short of an academic epidemic. At U.S. colleges, A's have surged from roughly 15 percent in 1960 to 43 percent by 2011, with private institutions leading the trend.[32] This is not only a problem at under-resourced institutions but also at the highest ranked institutions. Harvard's Office of Undergraduate Education released a 25-page report in 2025 showing that over 60 percent of student grades are now A's.[33] Harvard professor Steven Pinker noted that this has pushed the average grade-point-average (GPA) to around 3.6. The situation became so untenable that a new dean felt compelled to remind students that their primary obligation is education. As Pinker observed, the fact that such a reminder is necessary speaks volumes.[34]

There is a large body of scholarly literature showing that grades do not truly reflect learning, yet ironically, grade inflation is undermining the very career improvements that neoliberals claim market-driven education will deliver.[35] In that same interview, Pinker reported that after teaching essentially the same course for nearly 20 years, students' reading comprehension declined sharply.[36] The private sector, which neoliberals claim their approach to education serves, is feeling the cost. Mark C. Perna's 2025 *Forbes* piece underscores the harsh reality that employers, recognizing the skills gap, are spending thousands to train new hires.[37] And students are not unaware that they are not learning. Perna's piece also found that most recent graduates believe they learned more in six months of work than in four years of college.[38] Similarly, a month earlier an op-ed from a student in *The Harvard Crimson* argued that "It's Time for Harvard Students To Pick Up a Book," noting that students simply do not read.[39]

A documented rise in grade inflation has coincided with a campus culture that frames the college experience as a mere financial transaction. This environment communicates to students that paying tuition is the primary requirement for obtaining the commodity of a degree, rather than academic rigor. This shift has occurred during a period of education known as "The Great Disengagement."[40] Professor Patricia Zimmermann defines this phenomenon as a trend toward "college students who do not attend classes, fail to turn in their work, and refuse to participate in class discussions."[41] While some scholars argue this disengagement is a product of remote learning during the Covid-19 pandemic, others suggest it began decades earlier with the rise of smart devices, and some say even earlier.[42] In 1991, George Kuh and his colleagues described this dynamic as the "disengagement compact," a tacit bargain where faculty ask little of students, through easy grading and low workloads, while students, in turn, ask little of faculty, offering compliant behavior and favorable evaluations.[43] Regardless of the origin, educators in the classroom conclude that this lack of participation is detrimental to the quality of education. The coupling of rising marks and dwindling effort illustrates a paradox whereby students receive improved grades while faculty simultaneously bemoan a lack of meaningful engagement.

The institutional shift toward educators "serving" students, as management likes to say, has signaled to students that traditional academic participation is secondary to vocational outcomes. Zimmermann notes that many students now view reading, class participation, and theoretical courses as unimportant, choosing instead to focus on extracurricular activities, which they perceive as the "real" vocational training needed for employment.[44] From the student perspective, if they are passing their courses with minimal effort, there is little incentive to engage in academic work they find uninteresting. Furthermore, campus initiatives such as promotions for low-cost or free textbooks convey an effort to improve the affordability of the college experience but instead inadvertently reinforce the idea that scholarship lacks value, (though of course, lowering tuition is generally not an option). In a capitalist society where cost often symbolizes value, the push for free or low-cost materials can communicate that academic scholarship is essentially valueless. This environment—where teachers are expected to serve students, and "passing" is the only metric of a good "experience"— fosters an impression that the classroom is irrelevant. This is exemplified by students who attribute their success entirely to the instructor.

This transactional approach to education contributes significantly to broader psychological and cultural shifts among the youth. In 2009, Jean Twenge and W. Keith Campbell identified a "narcissism epidemic," which they define as a rise in inflated self-views and a sense of entitlement fueled by smart devices, easy credit, and cultural shifts toward self-admiration.[45] Education contributes to this epidemic by fostering the Dunning-Kruger effect, defined as a cognitive bias causing individuals with limited competence in a particular domain to overestimate their own abilities.[46] Many scholars argue that this is why so many people have increasing confidence in their ability to be content creators or influencers online: they believe they have original insights and speak with authority on subjects they do not truly understand.[47] The modern schooling system, by rewarding minimal effort with high marks, has helped foster this unearned confidence.

The rise of narcissism within the university system has transformed the nature of campus protest and intellectual engagement. During this era, many students began using protests to shut down speakers rather than engaging with their ideas. High-profile figures such as academic Richard Dawkins, television personality Bill Maher, and provocateur Milo Yiannopoulos faced cancellations due to resistance from University of California, Berkeley students.[48] While the media often framed these incidents as free speech issues, they actually highlight a deeper crisis of authority and intellectualism. It raises the question of why students feel they possess more authority on a subject than a seasoned researcher like Dawkins, or why an institution would invite a provocateur instead of hosting an accomplished scholar. Ultimately, these are the natural outcomes of a system in which education has been reduced to a mere commodity.

Passing Over Learning

When education becomes a commodity, the bottom line shifts from intellectual growth to customer satisfaction, and passing grades become the currency. It is rebranded as "student success," another corporate administrative buzzword that lacks agreed-upon meaning but is utilized to shut down substantive debate. In this environment, educational bureaucracy grows dense with rules that often conflict with logic, pedagogy, and common sense. These rules reward compliance rather than learning, creating an ecosystem where institutional procedures overshadow educational purpose.

Consider the Accommodations Office. These offices, variously labeled Disability Resource Centers or Accessibility Services, were originally designed to support students whose diverse abilities necessitated support in order for them to succeed in a traditional classroom. For example, a student with limited mobility may require a wheelchair; someone unable to write may need a note taker; a student with mental health challenges may rely on a service animal. I have encountered numerous students possessing critical thinking skills and compelling analysis who would not have succeeded had it not been for these accommodations. In principle, the goal is to ensure inclusivity by giving all students an equal opportunity to complete higher education. In practice, however, the question becomes: are these offices helping students who need support to learn, or merely helping students pass?

Recent research challenges the utility and necessity of certain accommodations granted to students. Studies show that students from wealthier districts tend to receive more accommodations.[49] Supporters argue this is because wealthier families have the resources to obtain proper diagnoses, while critics contend that wealthy parents use their resources to pressure schools into granting accommodations, giving their children a competitive edge in admissions. It is worth noting that scandals like the 2019 Varsity Blues case—wherein wealthy parents bribed their way into elite colleges facing financial pressures—demonstrate how affluent families use money to secure admissions for students who have not proven their academic merit, giving them an unfair advantage over more deserving students from less privileged backgrounds.[50] By the time students with accommodations reach higher education, their accommodations are transferred with them.

Among students, it is an open secret that the disability accommodations system is ripe for exploitation. In a 2026 article titled, "Nearly 40 percent of Stanford undergraduates claim they're disabled: I'm one of them," Elsa Johnson of Stanford University explained how students openly discuss strategies for obtaining unnecessary accommodations.[51] These "perks" range from assignment extensions and extra testing time to private dorm rooms. Johnson claims the process is easy: students simply feign conditions like depression, anxiety, "endometriosis," "ADHD, night terrors," or "gluten intolerance."[52] Because universities are desperate to avoid lawsuits regarding federal or state equal-access mandates, they grant these requests like candy. The statistics are striking: at Brown and Harvard, over 20 percent of undergraduates are registered as disabled; at Amherst College, more than 30%; and at Stanford, nearly 40 percent.[53] Meanwhile, at community colleges, only 3 percent to 4 percent of students receive such support.[54] Rose Horowitch described this phenomenon in education as "Accommodation Nation" in *The Atlantic.*[55]

When I shared this research with my own students, those with legitimate accommodations were the first to speak up. They expressed frustration with Johnson, fearing her article would further stigmatize those who truly need support. I clarified that her argument isn't against the existence of support for students with disabilities, but rather the "open secret" of system gaming. At this, many students chimed in to agree. Their justification, however, was cynical, "Our generation is so screwed, and we don't have universal healthcare, so we might as well get what we can." While most students I spoke to weren't particularly bothered by the practice of attaining accommodations under false pretense, a few expressed deep frustrations. They felt it was unfair to work hard for a passing grade while those gaming the system bragged about "going through the motions" without genuinely learning.

As a colleague of mine and I were bemoaning how some students with accommodations act entitled, she told me that after one of her courses concluded, a student who received an A in her course confided that he was homeless and juggling multiple jobs. My colleague remarked wryly, "How is it that a person living in their car can make it to class and turn in work on time, while my wealthier students have every accommodation and excuse for why the class is 'too hard' for them to succeed?" Indeed, the homeless student working multiple jobs is the type of student who should be getting support.

In my experience, those working in accommodations offices genuinely want to support students, but their job is to be compliant, not logical. For instance, in an online course I facilitated, students earned points for submitting their notes, a practice designed to improve retention that students consistently found valuable. In that same class, the accommodations office insisted that a student be assigned a peer note taker. To save money, the school wanted another student enrolled in the class to be the note taker. In exchange, the note taker would get early registration for courses. However, in order to avoid theft of another student's work, my syllabus explicitly prohibited students from submitting someone else's work as their own. I explained this to the accommodations office. They said that all they needed to do, to avoid legal complications, was show that the campus tried to get a notetaker. I compromised by requesting a volunteer from the class to be a notetaker, while warning that the volunteer who submitted notes would receive a zero, since that would constitute duplicate work. Unsurprisingly, no one volunteered. Equally unsurprising, the accommodations office was unbothered; they simply needed documentation that I had asked for a notetaker. Once their bureaucratic box was checked, their responsibility was fulfilled.

At times, certain mandated accommodations appear to prioritize passing over the actual mastery of the course material. For example, a new student entitled to "extended deadlines" rejected my proposal to make assignments available earlier. I assumed that they were entitled to an extended deadline because they needed more time to complete assignments than other students. However, the accommodation was for extended deadlines, meaning that the deadline itself was a problem rather than the time given. Unsurprisingly, the student repeatedly missed deadlines and ultimately failed the course. I then received numerous emails, clearly coordinated with the accommodations office, requesting an Incomplete, which allows up to a year to finish coursework. These interventions not only undermine time-management skills but also prevent students from developing basic communication abilities. Meanwhile, as a non-tenure-track instructor, I am not paid to grade work submitted months after the semester ends. In a system focused more on student retention than rigor, faculty labor often becomes an afterthought. I am not alone in recognizing the absurdity. Entire Reddit threads, such as "I believe in accommodations but do they become more questionable every year?" feature instructors trading strategies for navigating increasingly unreasonable demands.[56] Given the existence of grade inflation, the utility of accommodation beyond passing students is difficult to discern.

Conclusion

Education is not a consumer product: it is a public good that requires expertise, rigor, and professional judgment. Yet by privileging passing over learning, today's institutions undermine the very purpose of teaching. When students are conditioned to believe that their satisfaction or social comfort should supersede intellectual challenge, they leave college underprepared for professional, civic, and personal responsibilities. Faculty who resist these pressures face isolation, professional risk, and the demoralizing experience of watching years of training and expertise steadily devalued.

These internal trends do not remain hidden. The public sees them and grows skeptical. People increasingly question why their tax dollars should support institutions that invest in administrative bloat, ignore scholarship and expertise, and graduate students who seemingly learn little beyond how to file complaints when they feel uncomfortable. This perception—often oversimplified but rooted in visible dysfunction—shaped a significant portion of the electorate in 2016. Donald Trump capitalized on this skepticism, mocking higher education as an out-of-touch institution better suited for ridicule than for producing knowledge.

W When Trump took office in January 2017, I began the final term of my doctoral program; his election would unexpectedly become a defining influence on my career. I learned little from the course meetings that term, as the courses were effectively designed to shepherd me through a dissertation I had already completed. What I did not fully grasp at the time was that the program had taught me how to function as a scholar and administrator in a system already sealing its own demise. That collapse was still nearly a decade away, but the seeds had been planted, and they would grow under Trump's first term. How these years, especially the neoliberal response to Trump's Make America Great Again (MAGA) agenda, further accelerated the decline of higher education is the focus of the next chapter.

4

Performing Justice, Inviting Collapse

I had assumed Donald Trump would win the presidency in 2016, but I was not willing to say it publicly. As a working-class kid with roots in Kentucky and California, immigrant grandparents from Ireland, and an uncle with family from Mexico, I understood the deep appeal of Trumpism. It offered an alternative to the neoliberal economic policies that had ravaged the lives of working people. More important, Trump, ever the talented con man, promised that he, despite being a billionaire with no meaningful working-class ties, would "Make America Great Again" (MAGA) for ordinary Americans.

What I had not expected was academia's refusal to honestly confront the fact that the MAGA movement succeeded because the neoliberal agenda had failed. Instead, higher education elites dismissed Trump's rise to power as a fluke fueled by fake news, Russians, racists, sexists, and far-left "spoilers." Anyone who dared to suggest that real economic and cultural frustrations were driving his ascent was dismissed as "racist."[1] To be sure, Trump appealed to sexism and racism, but in that respect, he was not unique to American politics or the political right. What made Trump unique was that he campaigned against a Democratic Party that had not only abandoned the populist left, but successfully neutralized it.[2] Consequently, a decisive number of independents and former

Democrats, disillusioned by the status quo, surveyed America's two-party system and chose right-wing populism as their alternative.[3]

The Trump administration signaled a definitive departure from neoliberal norms in higher education, prioritizing nationalist and deregulatory agendas. A primary concern for the academic community was the intersection of the travel bans and the "Buy American, Hire American" executive order; these measures threatened the international enrollment and faculty staffing vital to institutional revenue and research continuity.[4] In a symbolic but controversial move, the administration transferred oversight of Historically Black Colleges and Universities (HBCUs) directly to the White House. Critics labeled the shift performative or racially insensitive, noting that it lacked the substantial federal funding increases—totaling billions in requested aid—that HBCU leaders argued were essential for survival.[5] Simultaneously, Secretary of Education Betsy DeVos championed "school choice" and sought to dismantle federal bureaucracy by rolling back Obama-era regulations on for-profit colleges.[6] This deregulatory stance culminated in the 2018 budget proposal, which sought a 13 percent reduction in Department of Education spending—a cut of approximately $9 billion. These fiscal contractions specifically targeted programs for low-income and first-generation students, while also reducing federal support for critical science and health research.[7]

Universities and colleges responded to these changes by doubling down on neoliberalism. They postured as "the resistance" to Trumpism arguing that the racist and sexist DNA of MAGA could be combatted with diversity, equity, and inclusion (DEI) policies and processes. World events, such as the Covid-19 pandemic, intervened. Trump's mishandling of the pandemic damaged his approval ratings and created an opening for neoliberal corporate agendas in higher education to be implemented with minimal resistance from traditional opposition groups, including faculty unions and students.

Although the pandemic offered neoliberal governance a momentary lifeline, it ultimately proved to be a Trojan horse. The pandemic-era narratives surrounding education, followed by the institutional responses to the post-October 7, 2023, campus protests, would serve as the final bow for the neoliberal project. This chapter explores how higher education's responses to Trumpism from 2016 to 2024 weakened the system and paved the way for the MAGA movement's 2025 goal: the eradication of higher education as we know it.

Trump's First Term

The final term of my doctoral program began in January 2017, just as Trump took office. Trump entered the White House after campaigning against higher education, having famously quipped "I love the poorly educated."[8] His attacks resonated with many Americans who felt that educated elites flaunted their cultural capital, pitied the poor with condescension, policed language, and demanded new norms such as pronoun sharing and land acknowledgments that felt imposed. Trump, famously attuned to a crowd, seized on that resentment by attacking college-educated people. Polls showed the more educated a voter was, the more likely they were to vote for Hillary Clinton.[9]

Neoliberals seemingly had no economic agenda for working people. All they offered were plenty of "corporate" trainings on how to teach working people to be less racist and sexist. The condescension in such approaches was excoriated by folks like University of California's Catherine Liu in *Virtue Hoarders*, which argues that neoliberal elites assume they possess the highest moral and intellectual virtue in language, sexuality, work, and taste; they maintain power by judging the "unenlightened" working class for lacking these virtues, even as they themselves often violate the standards they impose on others.[10]

Nothing better illustrates this perception than Larry Summers, a key architect of the corporatist, neoliberal turn in the administrations of Presidents Bill Clinton and Barack Obama. He advanced policies that sidelined talented regulators in the Clinton administration, such as Brooksley Born, who warned that the neoliberal economic theory of financial deregulation would enrich the wealthy and eventually crash the economy.[11] She was proven right when the 2008 financial crisis devastated poor and working-class communities that would later form a core part of Trump's base. Under Obama, with Summers once again in the White House, taxpayer dollars rescued the very institutions responsible for the collapse, while ordinary people were given little more than lectures about personal responsibility.[12] In the neoliberal imagination, aiding the rich is sound economic policy, while aiding the poor is dismissed as socialism.

Summers was rewarded with the presidency of Harvard University, where he presided over one of the nation's premier elite liberal institutions. Like many neoliberals, he openly suggested that his subjective notions of virtue guided how he ran the university. He denied tenure to Cornel West, an outspoken critic of neoliberalism and a black man, in part because he deemed West's participation in a rap album as "embarrassing" to Harvard.[13] Setting aside the racial contempt in the comment, Summers was signaling that, as an elite and wealthy college president, he believed he had the authority to define what was virtuous. Years later, documents from the late sex offender Jeffrey Epstein's files revealed that while Summers was lecturing West on virtue, he was suggesting that women had lower IQs than men.[14] Those files also described Epstein as Summers' "wing man" in securing sex from a "mentee" who, according to Summers, did not want the encounter but felt pressured by his power.[15] Summers was hardly an outlier; numerous academics at institutions such as Harvard and MIT maintained relationships with Epstein, as did many of the leaders of the investment firms that manage the multi-billion-dollar endowments of higher education institutions.[16] Nonetheless, Summers' behavior reveals a pathology of neoliberal elitism: a tendency to performatively signal virtues and principles that they neither genuinely held nor practiced, all while chiding the working class for failing to uphold the very standards that these elites habitually ignore.

This mindset also shaped higher education's response to Trumpism. In my own academic circles, merely suggesting that liberals might regain electoral viability by addressing working-class concerns was treated as racist or sexist. When I pointed out to a colleague that working-class whites found Trump appealing because he referenced that they were struggling desperately in the neoliberal economy, he responded, "That is ridiculous, no white people suffered." Similarly, a former student of mine, a Hispanic man who despised Trump, recalled being screamed at in class by his Black female professor at UC Berkeley simply for stating that Trump's election exposed deep societal rot. She believed that was heresy, as it gave legitimacy to Trump voters. The student told me that the only silver lining was that a few classmates defended him, though they were also shouted down. A little solidarity goes a long way.

During Trump's first term, it was commonplace for faculty to openly deride Trump supporters, including in our courses. The most jarring moment came when a colleague announced at a department meeting, "I've got one of those Trumpers in my class," prompting laughter and stories about wishing such students would "just drop [their class]" or "go away." Spencer Brayton and Natasha Casey documented the ease with which liberal educators felt empowered to dogmatically impose their electoral preferences on students; however, witnessing this phenomenon firsthand was truly chilling.[17] While it is the responsibility of educators to cultivate intellectual transformation, too many colleagues behaved as though such growth was impossible for certain students. If they truly believed that transformation was beyond reach, it begs the question: why were they in education at all?

The DEI Trap
Neoliberals believed that Diversity, Equity, and Inclusion (DEI) initiatives in higher education were the primary mechanism to

neutralize the ideological momentum of the MAGA movement. At first glance, DEI promised to build more just and inclusive campuses where historic discrimination is confronted. Historically, the academy was a fundamentally racist and exclusionary space, designed primarily to serve wealthy, white, male populations.[18] It is a striking irony that when higher education was intended almost exclusively for these groups, institutions were largely free and dedicated to a vision of the public good. However, integration coincided with the rise of the neoliberal academy; as student populations of color increased, state disinvestment followed, revealing a troubling correlation between changing demographics and a withdrawal of public funding.[19] This shift allowed administrators to oversee dramatically rising tuition and student fees, often to sustain their own inflated salaries rather than student success. The persistent suppression of student rights and the systemic failure to grant tenure to women of color reveal that the neoliberal agenda remains more concerned with institutional preservation than genuine equity.[20] Ultimately, the reality of this system is far more troubling than its inclusive rhetoric suggests.

The roots of DEI trace back to landmark civil rights victories such as *Brown v. Board of Education* (1954), which legally ended segregation in schools.[21] However, legal mandates did not dismantle structural inequality overnight. For example, discriminatory housing and economic stratification continued to segregate Northern schools. Affirmative action policies emerged in the 1960s and '70s as attempts to correct centuries of exclusion, opening doors for women and people of color.[22] Yet affirmative action became a political lightning rod, framed by conservatives who race-baited voters as "reverse discrimination" and weakened by Supreme Court rulings that outlawed racial quotas but allowed race as one admissions factor.[23] This political vulnerability prompted higher education to repackage affirmative action under softer terms: diversity, equity, and inclusion.[24] These concepts shifted emphasis from structural redress to symbolic representation.

It should be noted that DEI initiatives are vast in their focus and approach. However, it can be said that in higher education they operate from a neoliberal logic known as diversity ideology. Not to be confused with diversity, which seeks to "to engender tolerance, sophistication, and cosmopolitanism," diversity ideology seeks to diversify the privileged class—those with wealth, credentials, and positions of power—by adding more historically marginalized identities.[25] Champions of diversity ideology argue that the benefits that individuals derive from joining the privileged class will trickle down to others who share their identity. They also champion DEI policies and procedures that purport to diversify the curriculum, student body, faculty, and school administration to be more inclusive and equitable.[26] This is different from a material approach, which would give direct assistance or reparations to historically marginalized communities. Indeed, instead of raising revenue for marginalized communities by taxing the wealthy, providing reparations to historically oppressed groups, or offering cost-free services such as childcare or college tuition, DEI substitutes symbolic gestures for substantive redistribution. Instead, it extends opportunities in the form of college loans, burdens that marginalized communities can access only if they successfully navigate the challenges of neoliberalism up to age eighteen and then manage to attend college.

Beyond Buzzwords
While DEI advocates claim to perform anti-racist work, research suggests that the effectiveness of such training is complex. Although it can improve awareness, knowledge, and confidence in addressing racism, its ability to produce lasting behavioral or organizational change is widely debated and depends heavily on implementation.[27] Effective programs typically require a multifaceted, ongoing approach rather than a single session. However, rather than building an effective system, white liberals like Robin DiAngelo have commodified anti-racism by selling expensive workshops to

corporations and universities that rely on curricula derived from personal anecdotes rather than rigorous evidence.[28]

DiAngelo's book *White Fragility* sold millions of copies, yet it fails to challenge the structural systems that create racism. Instead, she locates the problem within individuals, insinuating that racism can be solved at the personal level rather than through a collective transformation of the system. Such a transformation would necessitate challenging those who benefit most from the current order, including corporate and university leadership. DiAngelo relies on her workshop experiences to conclude that white working people are inherently too "fragile" to discuss race; however, she neglects the fact that participants may feel uncomfortable discussing race openly because their managers are present. In such a high-stakes environment, any perceived misstep could jeopardize their careers.[29] Ultimately, DiAngelo provides exactly what neoliberals value: a moralistic framework that simplifies or silences complex realities while creating the illusion of progress.

DiAngelo is hardly alone. Without material solutions like reparations, DEI policies often serve as pacifiers, performative social justice that masks austerity, market logic, and growing inequalities tied to race, gender, class, sexuality, and ability. Research indicates that when universities define equity too narrowly, focusing only on internal campus demographics while ignoring their external footprint, the result is often detrimental to the broader community. In *In the Shadow of the Ivory Tower*, Davarian L. Baldwin argues that urban universities frequently drive gentrification and wage suppression in their surrounding neighborhoods. These institutional expansions and labor practices disproportionately harm Black and Latinx residents, effectively undermining the very equity goals the universities claim to champion.[30] Similarly, neoliberal frameworks often frame statistical data as "social justice victories" while obscuring underlying patterns of exploitation. For instance, institutions frequently celebrate DEI initiatives for increasing the representation of women and people of color within the academy.

However, these metrics often fail to disclose that a disproportionate number of these individuals occupy non-tenure-track positions, the most precarious and exploited labor class in higher education.[31] Furthermore, longstanding class inequities persist without mention, such as graduate students performing the bulk of the labor while faculty reap the rewards of research.[32]

Rather than engage with the shortcomings of their agenda, neoliberals typically rely on virtuous language and policies over substance. They contend that "student feelings" trump empirical data because, they argue, those who do not share the identity of the student cannot understand. This is known as relativism, the idea that there is no single, universal truth or moral standard. Instead, what people believe to be true or right depends on their personal experiences, cultural background, or the time and place they live in. As a result, what seems right to one group of people may seem wrong to another, with no agreed-upon standard for deciding which is correct. It is the epitome of a self-sealing fallacious argument. Kurt Andersen argues in *Fantasyland: How America Went Haywire (A 500-Year History)* that America's embrace of extreme "believe-whatever-you-want" thinking has blurred the line between fact and fiction, helping create a post-truth culture where personal belief often matters more than evidence.[33]

In relativist thinking, debates over discrimination become hierarchies of victimhood, sometimes known as the Oppression Olympics, where power becomes a metric for determining whose victimhood matters.[34] For example, I had a colleague once tell me not to confront a person of color who was accused of sexually harassing a white woman because white women have a history of making false accusations against people of color.
Because these terms have been stripped of their original meaning, neoliberal administrators can weaponize them as bureaucratic cudgels. This linguistic inversion is often used to justify institutional austerity. For example, during my transition to a new department, I was informed via email that I could not receive a salary increase

because "equity" required all new hires to start at the same base rate. This logic was applied despite the fact that my prior experience and publication record had already earned me merit-based raises in other departments within the same university.

Beyond theoretical debate, some researchers, notably philosopher Gabriel Rockhill in his 2025 book, *Who Paid the Pipers of Western Marxism?*, contend that ideological divisions in academia are intentional products of the intelligence community designed to fragment the Left. Rockhill argues that the U.S. Department of State and the Central Intelligence Agency (CIA) systematically co-opted critical theory during the Cold War, steering radical thinkers like Herbert Marcuse away from authentic Marxist materialist critiques and toward a "compatible left."[35] This sanitized version of leftist thought was restructured to serve U.S. interests by neutralizing its revolutionary potential and replacing class struggle with ideological subversion. According to Rockhill, Ivy League institutions functioned as recruiting grounds where this specific cohort was trained to reject communism and socialism in favor of a liberal-capitalist framework. Facilitated by state-operated and federally funded programs, this process effectively shaped an intellectual class that remains critical of the status quo while never challenging the foundational structures of capitalism.

These operations are not merely relics of the Cold War; in *Spy Schools* (2017), Daniel Golden argues that the intelligence community continues to exploit American universities in the post-9/11 era.[36] Golden reveals that the CIA, the FBI, and various foreign agencies have infiltrated nearly every level of academic life, enlisting everyone from tenured professors to undergraduates to serve as clandestine assets. This is supported in part by public records from the Department of Justice's investigation into Jeffrey Epstein. The files reveal that Epstein maintained connections with influential figures across news media, politics, finance, and academia. Within the educational sector, he was not merely a donor but was deeply integrated into the fabric of higher education, sustaining extensive ties with elite researchers and administrators. Furthermore, the records detail his frequent contact with individuals across various intelligence agencies, including those in the United States and Israel.[37] This overlap between academic funding, high-level intelligence, and billionaire influence provides a stark illustration of how neoliberal networks can bypass traditional institutional oversight.

Regardless of its origin or purpose, the managerial appropriation of social justice language has sparked an ironic and powerful right-wing backlash. Conservatives argue that DEI initiatives unfairly benefit minorities at the expense of white people. Though politically potent, this claim is largely unfounded. Neoliberals exploit this backlash by conflating all criticism of DEI with the conservative narrative, dismissing meaningful concerns as mere bigotry. This polarization strengthens ideological control within universities and silences dissenters, which include women and people of color across the ideological spectrum who critique DEI policies in education such as Zine Magubane, a professor of sociology and African American studies at Northwestern University; Coleman Hughes, a writer and philosopher; Adolph Reed Jr., a political scientist and professor emeritus at the University of Pennsylvania; Thomas Sowell, an economist and senior fellow at the Hoover Institution; and Cornel West, a philosopher, political activist, and professor of public philosophy at Harvard University.[38] I recall a colleague, whom I'll call Maverick, who questioned the evidence behind a campus climate report on race, which drew its conclusions based on a statistically insignificant sample size; he was effectively shunned from the community for daring to ask a question about the empirical legitimacy of a report.

From Justice to Bureaucracy
Rather than achieving genuine justice, DEI policies have frequently fostered a sprawling bureaucracy of managerial control. This shift has left faculty, many of whom recognize these systemic

shortcomings and abuses, with little recourse but to watch as administrative oversight supplants academic authority and fails to meet its own stated objectives. This dynamic is particularly evident in the evolution of how campus sexual misconduct is handled.

Title IX of the Education Amendments of 1972 is a federal civil rights law prohibiting sex-based discrimination in any educational program or activity receiving federal financial assistance.[39] It was designed to ensure equal opportunity in academics, athletics, and school activities, mandating specific procedures for handling sexual harassment, violence, and pregnancy discrimination; violations of these mandates can lead to the total withdrawal of federal funding. While Title IX's scope was expanded to include "sexual harassment" in the late 1970s, it was a 1992 U.S. Supreme Court ruling that authorized complainants to sue for damages if gender discrimination remained unresolved.[40] Also in the 1990s, the federal government had explicitly clarified that the prohibition of sex discrimination encompasses sexual harassment and assault, as such misconduct fundamentally impairs equal access to education.[41]

A pivotal shift occurred in 2011 when the U.S. Department of Education's Office for Civil Rights issued the "Dear Colleague" letter. This memo explicitly warned institutions that a failure to appropriately investigate and adjudicate cases of sexual harassment or assault could constitute a Title IX violation, thereby jeopardizing their federal funding.[42] Key provisions of the letter required a preponderance of the evidence standard for disciplinary action, a lower threshold than the clear and convincing standard often used previously, and mandated prompt investigations. Crucially, it prohibited schools from conditioning their internal disciplinary processes on the outcomes of the criminal justice system.[43]

Following this directive, powerful institutions faced mounting public pressure to address systemic sexual violence. This cultural climate reached a fever pitch in 2016 with the release of the *Access Hollywood* tape, which captured then-presidential candidate

Donald Trump boasting about sexual assault. This revelation, alongside investigative reporting on the systemic abuses of power by figures such as film producer Harvey Weinstein and television executive and media consultant Roger Ailes, catalyzed the #MeToo movement.[44] The #MeToo movement was a transformative social movement and awareness campaign aimed at exposing sexual abuse, sexual harassment, and rape culture. It created a collective space where survivors shared their personal experiences to demand accountability and social change. While the movement was originally founded by activist Tarana Burke in 2006, it reached an unprecedented global scale in 2017 when it sparked a worldwide conversation about systemic misconduct.[45]

The movement's scrutiny soon turned toward higher education, fueled by public outrage over the 2016 case of Brock Turner, a Stanford student caught in the act of assaulting an incapacitated woman. Turner's six-month sentence was widely condemned as shockingly lenient, highlighting a perceived disconnect between the gravity of the crime and institutional response.[46] A year earlier, the documentary *The Hunting Ground* alleged that campuses frequently concealed sexual assault to protect their reputations and endowments.[47] Subsequent films, such as the 2018 examination of the 2012 Steubenville, Ohio, gang-rape case, further illustrated a disturbing pattern: students accused of heinous crimes, particularly athletes viewed as revenue generators, often received minimal punishment or avoided accountability altogether.[48]

The resulting legitimate rage, when filtered through the PMC in higher education, yielded bureaucratic expansion. Instead of referring these reports to law enforcement, where they could be adjudicated in a court of law with the constitutional protections of due process, university administrations focused on hiring more staff, revising internal policies, and developing alternative resolution frameworks like "restorative justice." Critics contend these reforms have largely failed to prevent sex crimes or achieve true justice. Instead, they are often hamstrung by insufficient resources and the legal complexities of responding to "cold cases" involving former students.[49]

The core of the issue lies in the fact that these procedures empower the university to act simultaneously as judge, jury, and executioner. While schools are required to handle complaints internally with a different set of criteria than law enforcement, they generally maintain strict confidentiality, and reports to the police are often left to the discretion of the accuser rather than being made automatically by the institution.[50]

Many accusers decline to involve the police due to trauma or fear of retaliation, leaving the university as the primary investigator, a role that presents a fundamental conflict of interest.[51] Because public awareness of an epidemic of sexual assault is damaging to a university's brand and bottom line, institutions are incentivized to prioritize image management over transparency.[52] Title IX investigations are shielded from public view, and administrators often lack formal judicial training and the objectivity required for fair adjudication.[53] Ultimately, because it is in the university's best interest to avoid litigation or federal intervention, the system has incentivized a culture of "guilt by accusation" rather than a robust and objective due process.

In 2018, Rose Miron and Lena Palacios indicted the Title IX process in an article for the *Gender Report*, noting that "mandatory reporting policies protect universities, not survivors."[54] Given the opacity of this process, it is difficult to know how many survivors have been denied justice, or how many of the falsely accused were punished, simply to bolster the image that the university prioritizes accountability. In my time as an instructor, I have heard students express deep frustration regarding this lack of transparency, the denial of due process, and the absence of any genuine semblance of justice.

The public sympathy for these processes wore off as fast as they emerged. A 2016 documentary claiming that the woman who accused players on the Duke University lacrosse team of rape in

2006 was lying became a popularly used example to discredit accusers.[55] Furthermore, cases in which the #MeToo logic of "always believe the victim" was countered by people who believed some accusations, such as those against comedian Aziz Ansari, were conflating bad dates with sexual assault.[56] This led to public pressure to change federal support for #MeToo-era changes to sexual crime reporting on campuses.

In 2017, the Trump administration withdrew the 2011 "Dear Colleague" guidance, eventually replacing it in 2020 with formal, legally binding regulations. These new rules narrowed the definition of sexual harassment and restricted school jurisdiction primarily to on-campus activities. By requiring live hearings with cross-examination and allowing schools to adopt the higher "clear and convincing" evidentiary standard, these changes significantly enhanced due process protections for the accused.[57]

Critics rightly note that the traditional legal system has historically been biased against women and victims of sex crimes. Yet, allowing universities, which harbor clear conflicts of interest regarding their own reputations, to adjudicate these cases does not create an objective environment capable of delivering justice. In this sense, virtue signaling has often replaced substantive reform. Neither the "Dear Colleague" letter nor the post-2017 regulatory shifts solved the problem of holding the guilty accountable while securing justice for victims. The Obama administration's neoliberal approach prioritized victims even at the risk of punishing the innocent; conversely, the Trump administration's conservative agenda prioritized protecting the accused, even if it meant the guilty escaped accountability. In both frameworks, true justice remains elusive as long as the power to make these life-altering conclusions rests with unaccountable campus bureaucrats. While the Biden administration attempted to reverse these changes, its efforts were ultimately blocked by the courts in 2025, coinciding with the start of the second Trump administration.[58]

Covid-19:
The Pandemic of Opportunity and Discontent

"I have heard them say this on the news for so many other pandemics, such as Ebola and bird flu; I wouldn't worry about it." That is how I responded when a student expressed concern about the reporting on Covid-19 in March 2020. Two weeks later, the world shut down, and I found myself apologizing to that student. Suddenly, we were all told to teach from home. We were expected to use Zoom videoconferencing for class meetings and the learning management system Canvas for posting class materials and assignments. Having taught online and used videoconferencing for years, it was not a huge adjustment for me, but many faculty struggled.[59] Students explained how they were helping teachers learn the technology, while colleagues shared stories of essentially teaching other colleagues' courses because they did not understand the tech. Some people retired. What was supposed to last two weeks went on intermittently for three years. The first year was mostly remote, with a mix of shutdowns during virus surges in the final year or two, depending on the campus.

For educators, Covid-19 was a mixed bag in terms of how it impacted people's lives. On one hand, NTPT faculty could finally take a breath and avoid exhausting commutes, developing a better work-life balance. On the other hand, we were physically separated from our students and community, accelerating the corporatization of the classroom. The pandemic was a boon for Big Tech.

Pandemic Pedagogies

For more than a century, corporations have viewed students as a captive audience of untapped consumers. Companies ran contests like collecting cereal boxes or soup labels, offered prizes such as posters from their music labels, or donated money to schools in exchange for branding opportunities like putting their logos on gym scoreboards.[60] They also provided "free" products, including news broadcasts with advertisements for classroom use or MacBooks and tablets that collected student data for industry use. These efforts aimed to turn schools into opportunities to build brand loyalty, shape workforce preparation, and condition future consumers. Yet, despite industry's push for more involvement in the classroom, often promoted through neoliberal private-public partnerships under the guise of career readiness, faculty frequently resisted. They understood that academic freedom gave them not only control over the classroom, but a responsibility to not reduce education to socialization and marketization. Covid-19 changed that dynamic.

Emergency measures forced faculty to adopt corporate tools with little resistance, as concerns about privacy and copyright were set aside. The quick move to online education made it clear in no uncertain terms: educators would need to use corporate tools, if they wanted a career in higher education. Corporations not only entered schools; they reshaped education itself to serve their interests, turning students into products within a long-running experiment now culminating in AI and personalized learning.

The transition to remote learning was a major victory for Big Tech, granting unprecedented access to classrooms and vast streams of faculty and student data. Education shifted into a production line model wherein students are treated less as developing citizens and more as data points to be mined, nudged, and profiled. These companies embedded surveillance tools into homes and classrooms, normalizing invasive monitoring disguised as innovation. This constant data collection built detailed, permanent profiles of students that follow them beyond graduation, all hidden behind opaque consent agreements. Despite the tools' claims to enhance students' education or safety, the true beneficiaries are corporations that profit from commodifying student information.[61] Worse, the culture of surveillance undermined learning, as studies show that students are less likely to ask questions or share openly when they know they are being watched.[62] This harmed the educational process, which relies on students making mistakes and learning from them. Teachers were unwitting participants in this system, using software that tracks engagement rather than encouraging critical thinking. Every assignment fueled corporate databases, feeding AI models that would later judge student work.

The shift to remote learning also revealed how neoliberal commitments to DEI rhetoric collided with the profit-driven priorities of corporate education. Research shows that surveillance technologies disproportionately harm historically marginalized communities. Big Tech products are trained on biased data that reflect the assumptions of their creators, which helps explain why students of color are disproportionately flagged for criminal behavior, trans students for mental health concerns, and disabled students for cheating.[63] These false accusations compound existing educational barriers, as tools marketed as making education more objective and efficient instead introduce new forms of inequality and harm. Institutions themselves often weaponize data to protect their own interests against students. For example, a number of universities have defended themselves in court against allegations that they failed to protect students from sexual assault by introducing the accusers' university counseling records.[64]

Fear and Favor of a Pandemic
During the pandemic, fear was utilized by the PMC to steamroll resistance from faculty unions and students against growing corporate control of the classroom. At that time, universities mandated vaccinations for reopening, assuming the vaccine would entirely prevent symptoms and cause no significant side effects – a premise that proved flawed or debatable.[65] The larger issue was whether employers should have the authority to require vaccines as a condition of employment.

Although I supported vaccination personally, I opposed the mandates because they handed excessive power to administrators. While serving on an academic freedom committee, I cautioned that vaccine mandates could intimidate faculty from controversial research or lectures. Instead of engaging with this concern, a history professor dismissed it with a rehearsed pro-vaccine speech echoing MSNBC liberal talking points and ignored the real threat to academic freedom. As a media scholar married to a scientist, I witnessed distorted pandemic narratives spread by both liberal and conservative media. While fully vaccinated and double-boosted, I was frustrated by faculty parroting partisan oversimplifications instead of nuanced science. Compared to my colleagues, scientists I knew offered more accurate and sophisticated perspectives on lockdowns, vaccine effects, and side effects.

The ideological agenda in higher education had no place for such substantive analysis. Institutions placed their absolute trust in bureaucratic experts like Dr. Anthony Fauci—Director of the National Institute of Allergy and Infectious Diseases (NIAID) from 1984 to 2022 and later Chief Medical Advisor to the President— despite his repeated admissions to misleading the public. Early in the pandemic, for instance, Fauci discouraged masking, later explaining that he withheld the truth to prevent a shortage of personal protective equipment (PPE) for first responders.[66] Similarly, in December 2020, he admitted to incrementally nudging the reported percentage required for herd immunity based on his perception of what the public was ready to hear.[67] This pattern extended to 2021, when he attempted to persuade unvaccinated individuals by claiming the vaccine would ensure they experienced "no symptoms" upon contraction. Such claims proved demonstrably false, as the Centers for Disease Control and Prevention (CDC) and research scientists eventually confirmed that vaccinated individuals could still experience symptoms and transmit the virus.[68]

While some justify these contradictions as necessary for public health, dismissing critics who identified these inconsistencies as "conspiracy theorists" only deepened skepticism toward the expert class and the broader public health agenda. Indeed, figures like Joe Rogan—who was himself famously and inaccurately accused by CNN of consuming "horse dewormer"—capitalized on these institutional failures to build a massive, loyal audience for his podcast.[69] Simultaneously, social media platforms suppressed the "lab leak" theory, often labeling suggestions that the virus originated in a Chinese laboratory as inherently xenophobic or "racist."[70] Years later, however, various U.S. intelligence agencies and scientific bodies would acknowledge the lab leak as a credible, if not likely, possibility. Within higher education, merely entertaining this hypothesis was often treated as a career-ending transgression. For example, one faculty member teaching propaganda at a prestigious university used Covid-19 as an example of how propaganda is constructed. He was reported to the campus by a student who was said to feel uncomfortable with an instructor discussing Covid-19 narratives as propaganda. This clear violation of academic freedom nearly led to the educator being fired. Furthermore, it serves as a stark illustration of the chilling effect induced by the pandemic. While neoliberal voices in media and academia ignored these critiques and controversies, Rogan and his guests openly dissected them. This process ultimately delegitimized traditional authorities while positioning decentralized media platforms as the primary arenas for 'unauthorized' truth and heterodox inquiry.

Despite the climate of widespread fear, many liberals found themselves tied in rhetorical knots as they attempted to signal virtue at the cost of consistency. Following the brutal murder of George Floyd by Minneapolis police, a resurgence of Black Lives Matter (BLM) activism drew large numbers of both white liberals and conservatives into the streets.[71] These mass demonstrations occurred shortly after neoliberal commentators had demonized working-class protesters in Michigan for violating Covid-19 lockdown protocols to demand an economic reopening. To reconcile this apparent hypocrisy, proponents argued that BLM participants practiced rigorous masking and social distancing, whereas the Michigan protesters did not.[72] However, these claims were often made without the support of substantive comparative data or longitudinal analysis, relying more on narrative preference than epidemiological proof.

In higher education, neoliberals responded to the BLM movement by advocating for Critical Race Theory (CRT) in schools. I have used this theory in my work and classroom.[73] CRT is an accepted academic theory, which means it has been tested and refined. It argues that systems developed by white people serve white interests through seemingly race-neutral processes or language. In effect, these systems are racist.

In one meeting, a faculty member conflated CRT with culturally relevant pedagogy, an educational approach empowering students by using their cultural backgrounds, experiences, and knowledge as assets to achieve academic success.[74] The faculty member argued that "we need to teach Black history in every class." However, the inclusion of more examples of people of color and their history is part of culturally relevant pedagogy, not necessarily CRT. Tensions came to a head during a similar meeting at another campus when a group of faculty proposed mandating CRT in every course, a clear violation of academic freedom. Like any academic theory, CRT belongs only in relevant courses, just as the theory of gravity is not mandated in every speech course. These were the embarrassing conversations behind closed doors. Covid-19 allowed the public to get a deep look into how ridiculous corporatism had made higher education.

Higher Education Embarrassed

During the pandemic, internet use surged as audiences watched the transition of power from Trump, who appeared unable to control the crisis, to Joe Biden. The violent spectacle of January 6, 2021, when rioters who accepted Trump's baseless claim that the 2020 election was stolen attempted and failed to overturn the election outcome, captured the public's imagination during the lockdown.[75] Outside of politics, the pandemic brought education and campus culture into sharper public focus and fueled heated cultural debates. In news media, the debates over vaccines, school reopenings, and CRT raged, with the public discussing public education in a way that I had not seen.

Simultaneously, the shift to remote schooling allowed parents and the broader public to monitor classrooms and attend virtual school board meetings. This unprecedented transparency sparked a wave of ridicule, criticism, and disdain toward the modern educational curriculum. Some prominent voices on the Left even joined the critique. Matt Taibbi published a scathing essay that blamed critical pedagogy for the decline of higher education.[76] Intellectually, the essay was nonsense, as he seemed not to understand the critical scholarship he was condemning, particularly the work of Marcuse. His ignorance of higher education was revealed when he conflated administrators and faculty, as well as neoliberals and leftists, in his analysis. Nonetheless, his argument fed public cynicism about academia.

The criticisms did not come just from the Left. The pandemic gave audiences the idea that discussions about race in America had grown in a nonsensical direction with the publications of academic talks on race. One of the most prominent examples was a talk at Yale University titled "The Psychopathic Problem of the White Mind," by Dr. Aruna Khilanani. In the talk, which was on Zoom due to pandemic restrictions, Khilanani noted, "Nothing makes me angrier than a white person who tells me not to be angry. White people make my blood boil. I had fantasies of unloading a revolver into the head of any white person that got in my way, burying their body and wiping my bloody hands as I walked away relatively guiltless with a bounce in my step, like I did the world a f——-ing favor."[77] The talk was ridiculed as evidence that the Left's obsession with race was insanely out of control. People of color such as Coleman Hughes joined the fray arguing that this was unacceptable for anyone of any racial identity to express.[78]

Much of what people were seeing seemed to confirm what popular podcasters such as Rogan had been warning about. Rogan hosted figures from the so-called "intellectual dark web" such as

Jordan Peterson, who built a career attacking political correctness in higher education, and Eric Weinstein, who portrays academia as broken and conspiratorial. Rogan amplified the notion that universities had become corrupt ideological machines rather than spaces for learning, debate, or professional development.[79]

These voices challenged progressive academic ideas and drew attention to contentious campus events, including the "Day of Absence" controversy at Evergreen State College in Washington, which drew attention to Weinstein's brother and sister-in-law, Professors Bret Weinstein and Heather Heying.[80] The event, an annual tradition for students and faculty of color to meet off-campus, sparked controversy when the plan changed to ask white people to voluntarily stay off campus in a show of solidarity. Weinstein opposed the new version of the event, which was mischaracterized as mandatory, and his email protesting the change led to backlash and his eventual resignation. He was lionized as a victim of liberal higher education, a rallying cry for conservative critics of these institutions.

The episode led to internet discussion and derision of "safe spaces" on campus. Safe spaces are designated areas on campus intended to provide individuals, especially those in marginalized groups, with an environment free from discrimination, harassment, or offensive speech, where they can express themselves without fear of judgment or harm. However, these safe spaces became great fodder for comedians who mocked their use, arguing that higher education had devolved into little more than an expensive opportunity to be shielded from academic critique and reassured in one's preexisting worldview.

The internet also got a laugh at the expense of higher education with the performative language of Stanford University's short-lived Elimination of Harmful Language Initiative.[81] The initiative sought to remove racist, violent, and biased language from university websites and code, but it drew swift criticism for including words like "American," "immigrant," "grandfather," "brave," and even "hip-hip-hooray" as potentially harmful. Some substitutions were equally absurd: "take a shot at" became "give it a go"; "no can do" became "I can't do it"; and "submit" was deemed a harmful term.[82] The backlash was immediate, prompting Stanford first to hide the guide and ultimately to remove it entirely.[83] The university acknowledged the good intentions of staff who had created the initiative but clarified that the list never represented official policy, underscoring the fine line between promoting inclusivity and descending into performative overreach.[84]

Other academics took a deliberately academic approach to illustrate what they saw as the neoliberal orthodoxy on college campuses in what became known as the "Grievance Studies Affair." This academic hoax, which was also platformed on Rogan's podcast, exposed ideological bias in certain fields by submitting absurdist papers on topics like gender and race to scholarly journals, including some on "dog rape."[85] Academics Helen Pluckrose (MA in early modern studies), James A. Lindsay (PhD in mathematics), and Peter Boghossian (assistant professor of philosophy) submitted papers with titles such as "The Conceptual Penis as a Social Construct," focusing on "rape culture," and deliberately using incoherent language full of social justice terminology. By the time the hoax was exposed, four of the papers had been published, three more accepted, and several were under review. They concluded that this proved that academia had become more focused on virtue signaling than scholarship. These experiences mirror larger academic controversies such as the 1996 Sokal Affair, when physicist Alan Sokal submitted a deliberately nonsensical paper to the cultural studies journal *Social Text* to reveal ideological favoritism over scholarly rigor. I witnessed how political virtue signaling triumphed over scholarship firsthand in my own field as both an editor and a writer, when reviews began including subjective critiques rather than scholarly ones.[86]

The election of President Joe Biden gave higher education renewed confidence that they had been right all along, viewing Trump as an aberration. However, signs were emerging that people's faith in education, and by extension, the Democratic Party, was fading. Polls showed that for the first time, Democrats were losing support on education, an issue they had held a near monopoly over for decades.[87] An off-year victory by Republicans in the Virginia governor's race was understood to be a result of voter frustration with neoliberal education policies.[88] Even Biden's effort to address the economic concerns of working people by alleviating student debt through the Saving on a Valuable Education (SAVE) program backfired: opponents criticized it as a government handout to college-educated elites funded by working-class taxpayers, while supporters argued it failed to address the structural issues driving tuition increases.[89] Despite their battered reputation, institutions believed that staying the course was the best path forward. With vaccines being administered and mandates in effect, administrators aggressively moved to convince faculty and students to come back to in-person learning. Then, with Biden in office, on October 7, 2023, everything changed.

Gaza:
The Final Nail in Higher Education's Coffin

The political firestorm began with the deadly attacks in Israel on October 7, 2023. They were carried out by Hamas, a Palestinian Sunni Islamist political and militant movement that has governed the Gaza Strip since 2007. The attack included a barrage of at least 4,300 rockets and coordinated incursions by vehicles and powered paragliders. By the time the violence ended, nearly 1,200 people were killed and 251 hostages were taken.[90] Israel's response, framed as an effort to capture the perpetrators and free the hostages taken by Hamas during the attack, resulted in an estimated 70,000 to 100,000 Palestinian deaths and left hundreds of thousands injured and facing starvation by October 2025.[91] President Joe Biden and Congress provided full support for Israel's actions in Gaza, supplying over $20 billion in funding and weapons for the Jewish state.[92] Yet, unlike previous causes such as BLM or Ukraine, higher education was not united behind the Democratic Party's approach to Israel.

(De)Activating Campus Activism
The turning point came in April 2024, when Columbia students launched a Gaza solidarity encampment demanding divestment from Israel, financial transparency, and amnesty for activists.[93] The students' decision to react with protest was unsurprising. After all, over the previous two years, they had seen campus statements and email signatures from faculty and administrators showing their solidarity with BLM and Ukraine in its war against Russia. Instead of engaging responsibly with the encamped students, administrators at Columbia University called in the New York Police Department, resulting in the arrest of more than 100 students and the removal of the encampment.[94]

Columbia University had been experiencing pressure from supporters of Israel such as alumni groups, trustees, politicians, and the news media.[95] Indeed, the news media largely remained uncritical of Israel during the first eighteen months of its assault in Gaza. Media scholar Robin Andersen, for instance, documented how content and individuals critical of Israel were removed from American news outlets.[96] Simultaneously, politicians blamed TikTok and other social media platforms for cultivating sympathy for Gazans among young people. These claims ultimately led to efforts to ban TikTok in the U.S., as it had emerged as the primary platform not censoring content critical of Israel.[97] Relatedly, many in politics and news media, most notably Bill Maher, denounced higher education, arguing that universities had made young people so "stupid" that they felt sympathy for the plight of Gazans.[98] Columbia's actions marked only the beginning, as over 100 encampments soon appeared on college campuses nationwide, and would meet similar resistance from university leadership.[99]

Administrators across the nation justified their crackdown on encampments and protests as an effort to maintain "safety" and ensure a "diverse" community.[100] They argued that criticism of Israel was inherently antisemitic and therefore tantamount to "hate speech." It should be noted, however, that hate speech is protected under the U.S. Constitution.[101] Attempts to restrict hate speech have faced legal challenges and criticism from free speech groups like the American Civil Liberties Union (ACLU).[102] What complicates restricting hate speech is subjectivity: some claim that criticizing Zionism is antisemitic, and thus a form of hate speech, while others argue that opposing a political ideology such as Zionism or the actions of a nation such as Israel is not, in itself, hate. Nonetheless, deeming such criticism and protests as forms of hate was used by the PMC to justify police raids that sparked violence and led to arrests at campuses such as the University of California, Los Angeles;[103] censoring student groups for promoting pro-Palestinian discourse at Indiana University and the University of Texas at Austin;[104] and unilaterally canceling graduation and moving final exam week to online learning.[105] UC Berkeley, a campus historically celebrated for its free speech legacy, was designated a "Hostile Campus" by the Council on American-Islamic Relations, California (CAIR) precisely because it punished and stigmatized students who showed sympathy for the people of Gaza.[106] A commission of leading United Nations human rights watchdogs sent letters condemning the presidents and provosts of Columbia, Cornell, Georgetown, Minnesota State, and Tufts Universities, stating that the crackdowns on and treatment of pro-Palestinian students constituted human rights abuses.[107]

The Feckless Faculty

On many campuses, the decision to support the right to protest divided administrators and faculty. Many neoliberals viewed it as enabling antisemitism, while more progressives saw it as upholding constitutional rights and freedoms.[108] For example, at one campus, administrators attempted to suppress dissent by making it illegal to send emails discussing "non-work-related issues" after colleagues circulated op-eds on the conflict. Only a minority of faculty protested. I raised my concern during a faculty meeting and two tenured faculty members, Frederick and Napoleon, disagreed with me and lectured me on how shutting down email communication was justified because "this is different than writing about BLM; it's a foreign conflict." I interrupted to point out, "So was Ukraine," but they ignored me. On the Academic Freedom Committee at another campus, I witnessed the tenured professor serving as committee chair effectively shut down faculty responses critical of the campus decision to dismantle encampments.

Faculty were feckless in part because they were afraid. Their collective bargaining power had been so severely weakened that, across the nation, numerous faculty members—most notably the vulnerable NTPT—were being suspended or fired for supporting campus protests, despite protections under Title VI of the Civil Rights Act, which grants the federal government authority to investigate antisemitism.[109] While some eventually regained their positions, by then the damage had been done. The fear had spread, which helped explain why I couldn't even rally a group of faculty to demand that the campus release the data on reported antisemitism used to justify the shutdown. Many colleagues declined out of fear; some even worried the data might support the crackdown—an astonishing admission of intellectual cowardice. Were they truly afraid to reconsider their views based on evidence? Or were they afraid to find that the campus was weaponizing antisemitism to justify the restriction of rights? I suspect I'll never get an answer.

To be sure, antisemitic rhetoric appeared on college campuses and across the nation.[110] Administrators' commitment to combatting hate seemed selective. Research would later show that incidents of harassment against Arab and Muslim students in 2024 following October 7, 2023 were on par with what Jewish students experienced.[111] According to CAIR-California's reporting, UC Berkeley had one of the highest rates of Islamophobic harassment in the state: 85 percent of Muslim students reported harassment, 88 percent said they were targeted by peers due to religious identity,

and 71 percent reported being unfairly singled out by faculty—
nearly double the statewide average.[112] This occurred in a climate
where political and media figures were justifying Israel's actions in
Gaza, which the United Nations called a "genocide," by saying
"Israel has a right to defend itself."[113] However, Arab and Muslim
students did not receive the same outcry of support from
administrators, illustrating that the campus crackdowns were more
focused on signaling their support for the neoliberal agenda in
relation to Israel than actually protecting students from harassment.

Conclusion:
The 2024 Election

The post–October 7th environment exposed the ineptitude
and anti-democratic nature of higher education institutions. In
December 2023, members of the United States Congress began
convening televised congressional hearings to investigate the
ongoing campus protests. During one such hearing, the presidents of
Harvard University, the University of Pennsylvania, and the
Massachusetts Institute of Technology were subjected to aggressive
questioning by Representative Elise Stefanik regarding the origins
and underlying causes of the demonstrations. Rather than offer a
moral justification, they did what the PMC does, relying on legal
justification to perform damage control. One commentator described
it as bringing "a book to a knife fight."[114] Their answers were seen
by many as "evasive," "feckless," and lacking "moral clarity" from
both supporters and opponents. Indeed, they relied on the same
process-related arguments that had led me to refer to our campus
polices as "Un-American," when I was speaking to Farley, whom we
met in the Introduction to this book.

As a result, within weeks, Penn's Elizabeth Magill and
Harvard's Claudine Gay resigned under pressure from donors and
lawmakers. The message to university leaders was clear: suppress
pro-Palestinian speech or risk losing your job. In effect, the top-

113

down neoliberal model of governance—much like CEOs answering to their boards—had delivered its final decree. Higher education at the end of 2024 was a landscape of fiefdoms: university presidents followed executive orders, students paid for restricted rights, and faculty, paralyzed by fear, waited for the next superficial initiative. This was the hollowed-out shell that Donald Trump prepared to crush—a topic explored in the next chapter.[115]

5

Building
The MAGAcademy

"You all need some public relations help," Lisa declared from the stage. Standing before an audience in Washington, D.C., she was voicing the uncomfortable truth we all knew: the public had lost faith in higher education. It was three months into President Donald Trump's second term, and our 2025 conference had gathered academics and practitioners across media, politics, and history to discuss character assassination. Lisa was the picture of poise, exuding the kind of expertise that commanded immediate respect. As a high-level public relations (PR) strategist for a major firm, she made it clear her clientele included the famous and the powerful, none of whom she would be naming. Her critique was gentle but firm; while she didn't dwell on the details, her message to my profession was unmistakable: your image is in shambles. That same year, a Gallup survey found that only about one-third of adults now view a college education as "very important," a 15-year low and a steep drop from 75 percent in 2010 and 51 percent in 2019.[1] This decline spans all demographic groups, including age, race, gender, and political affiliation, with notable dips among women, people of color, and college graduates. Less than half of degree holders now feel their education was worth the cost.[2] The erosion of confidence reflects multiple concerns, including the high cost of college, perceptions that institutions are politically biased, doubts about practical job preparation, and the rise of alternative pathways such as trade schools and microcredentials.

Public distrust in higher education now reflects a wider skepticism toward the Democratic Party and its academic-leaning agenda. By 2025, the two major political parties in the U.S. had bifurcated, with polls showing someone with a college degree was much more likely to be a Democrat than a Republican.[3] In late 2025, the favorability of the Democratic Party hit a near three-decade low.[4]

For decades, conservatives had viewed higher education as a primary obstacle to their political goals, convinced that universities functioned as indoctrination centers for the Democratic Party. Now, Trump was poised to dismantle this perceived threat once and for all. Playing into the online lampoonist interpretation of diversity, equity, and inclusion (DEI) policies, Trump portrayed higher education on the campaign trail as a political battleground where victory needed to be reclaimed from the so-called "woke" left.[5] Originally, "wokeness" referred to an awareness of social injustices and systemic inequality, but over time, the term had been twisted into a derogatory label used to mock what critics saw as the excesses and absurdities of identity politics, especially as they related to DEI policies in higher education.[6] Worse still, polls revealed that this negative use of "woke" resonated with voters across the ideological spectrum, many of whom, having lived through the upheavals of the Covid-19 pandemic and the Gaza conflict, viewed higher education not as a place of knowledge production and serious people, but as a cartoonish environment where ridiculous ideas about race and gender were treated with legitimacy.

Capitalizing on voter frustration, Trump's second term launched a systemic assault designed to reshape higher education into the MAGAcademy. Trump's second-term policies on education were a coordinated, systematic campaign to weaken American educational institutions, consolidate federal control, and impose a politically driven ideology. This was achieved through a strategic battery of executive orders, federal investigations, and the systematic dismantling of the Department of Education. Beyond policy, the administration encouraged the targeted intimidation of political enemies on campus, creating an environment where the looming threat of losing funding, employment, or legal status pressured everyone to self-censor.

What made it particularly striking is how closely, both rhetorically and in practice, Trump's agenda relied on neoliberal logic. He framed privatization as a necessary solution to "wasted" taxpayer money.[7] He invoked inclusivity and opposition to bigotry as a rationale for zero-tolerance policies that homogenized campus curricula and culture. He fetishized technology as a pretext for expanding so-called artificial intelligence (AI) in education. He portrayed faculty as unprofessional and inefficient, in need of the motivational force of the market. Neoliberals had primed the public to buy these arguments and solutions. The tools and ideology were there; Trump utilized them for his own purposes.

By 2025, students and faculty, overworked, exhausted, isolated, alienated, and divided, could offer little resistance. Years of division, corporatization, and administrative power had created an academic community unprepared to fight. Worse, neoliberal governance had handed Trump the very tools he needed to transform higher education. For years, liberals had used funding for DEI as carrots to extract concessions from institutions. Trump simply replaced the carrot with a conservative content and policies. Similarly, neoliberals had used investigations about DEI violations to justify funding cuts and ideological homogeneity; Trump employed similar tactics under the banner of combatting antisemitism. Just as neoliberals had long invoked budgets and market pressures to justify the expansion of NPTP (non-tenure-track/part-time) faculty positions, Trump used the same economic rationale to justify the deprofessionalization of certain fields and disciplines. Building on a neoliberal legacy of restricted free speech, Trump launched a fresh offensive against campus activism. The irony was thick: after years of steamrolling dissent from within, universities were now being steamrolled by the state. Suddenly, administrators were in the awkward position of begging the very students and faculty they had once marginalized to stand on the front lines for them.

Trump was building the MAGAcademy. Within this ecosystem of enforced conformity, the looming threat of losing funding, employment, or legal status compelled everyone—from executive-level decision-makers to students and faculty—to sanitize every facet of academic life, from institutional policy and public communication to the very nature of their research. In the MAGAcademy, leftist ideologies are treated as tantamount to treason. Any attempt to address or resolve historical inequities, deep-seated prejudices, or human rights abuses in the United States is strictly verboten. This is the MAGAcademy, an authoritarian evolution made possible by a neoliberal era that hollowed out higher education and left it vulnerable to this swift implementation. Where Trump lacked the preparation to effectively exert power during his first term, his second term marked an administration that was highly organized and laser-focused on implementing his agenda, especially regarding education. By the end of the first year of Trump's second term, the corporate authoritarianism built over decades had been firmly weaponized against higher education.

The War on Woke

Conservatives had long viewed higher education as an oppositional institution to their political project. For example, the president of the conservative Heritage Foundation, Kevin Roberts, bemoaned the fact that his conservative ideology was suppressed during his time at New Mexico State University. He described being excluded from a symposium on Ronald Reagan because colleagues allegedly feared his "facts." He also claimed he was prevented from pursuing scholarship on African American history because of his identity as a white male.[8]

In addition to Roberts' qualms, there was also a hefty amount of conservative literature that argued that academics were anti-American, such as *The Professors: The 101 Most Dangerous Academics in America* by David Horowitz (2006) and *Illiberal Education: The Politics of Race and Sex on Campus* by Dinesh D'Souza (1991).[9] However, no one did more to excoriate the character of higher education than Charlie Kirk, the prominent right-wing social media provocateur and founder of Turning Point USA. Kirk created an empire by producing online videos in which he antagonized college students on their campuses for what he saw as their lack of knowledge in higher education, flaunting his critiques under the banner of free speech.[10] Kirk's content framed higher education as an obsolete investment for the younger generation. By positioning conservative influencers like himself as the primary sources of intellectual authority, he argued that traditional academic institutions had lost their monopoly on knowledge.

Trump immediately focused on appeasing conservative critics of higher education by delivering on his campaign promise to "combat wokeness." His goal was to eliminate "woke, socialist, and anti-American ideology" from American universities.[11] Within his first week, he issued a series of sweeping executive orders that reversed Title IX protections for transgender students, banned DEI programs across federal agencies, and empowered federal officials to investigate compliance with these mandates.[12] In addition, he rolled back a Biden-era DEI initiative that replaced Times New Roman font with the reportedly more accessible Calibri.[13] The administration weaponized the legal definition of discrimination, contending that programs at Minority-Serving Institutions (MSIs) were "unlawful" because they supposedly privileged specific racial groups over others.[14] Additional executive orders barred celebrations of cultural awareness months and restricted the use of federal resources for diversity-related events.[15] He also made it more difficult to prosecute discriminatory practices by repealing disparate impact liability, a policy that holds entities accountable for facially neutral actions that, while not intentionally discriminatory, disproportionately harm protected groups.[16]

Trump's "war on woke" in higher education centered heavily on gender and sex. His administration issued orders requiring that sex be recognized strictly as biological male or female, effectively rolling back legal protections for transgender students.[17] Simultaneously, the capacity of the Office for Civil Rights (OCR) was severely diminished; its staff was halved and seven of its twelve regional offices were shuttered.[18] These administrative cuts and a perceived lack of empathy illustrate the risks of placing investigations of these offenses in the hands of bureaucrats rather than a judicial system rooted in due process and established concepts of justice. *Inside Higher Ed* reported that federal data reveals a staggering decline in enforcement: in all of 2025, the OCR "resolved zero complaints of sexual harassment or violence" and has "opened fewer than 10 sexual violence investigations since March 2025."[19]

Trump's anti-woke agenda in higher education was inseparable from a broader effort to purge immigrants and non-white populations. Having built his political career on scapegoating immigrants for social and economic decline—including promoting racist conspiracy theories such as that President Obama was not a U.S. citizen, known as birtherism, or that Mexico was only sending criminals to the U.S., or that immigrants were eating people's pets[20]—Trump moved to make colleges and universities hostile terrain for undocumented and precariously documented students by stripping campuses of their "sensitive location" protections against immigration enforcement.[21] The authorization of warrantless campus raids and arrests has effectively barred students with contested immigration status from safely accessing higher education.[22] This climate of fear was intensified by a Supreme Court ruling authored by Brett Kavanaugh that sanctioned immigration stops, known by critics as "Kavanaugh stops," which are based only on perceived race, ethnicity, language, or occupation.[23] The criteria for detention became dangerously broad: anyone who fit a subjective profile of an 'undocumented immigrant' was at risk of being swept up by authorities. Worse, many ed-tech tools normalized during Covid-19 continue to collect and track student data, which the federal government can and does access to pursue migrants.[24] As a result, schools increasingly function as unsafe spaces for students who are themselves undocumented or who live with people whose immigration status is contested.

Trump framed these reforms as an effort to promote "intellectual diversity," but in practice, they served as a mechanism for enforcing ideological homogeneity.[25] By directing the DOE and the Department of Justice (DOJ) to investigate unlawful discrimination, a thinly veiled directive to dismantle DEI initiatives, the administration effectively criminalized institutional efforts at inclusion, replacing them with a singular, state-sanctioned viewpoint.[26] Similarly, on the campaign trail he promised to reform the accreditation process, which is the process by which agencies review schools and programs to ensure they meet standards for quality education. During the campaign, Trump vowed to replace the "radical left" and "Marxist lunatic" accreditors with those promoting "American tradition" and "Western civilization."[27] As of late 2025, his administration was implementing a plan to overhaul accreditation.[28] Furthermore, he threatened to withhold funding from institutions that considered sex and race in admissions and that did not define gender based on male or female sex at birth.[29]

To realize the MAGAcademy, the Trump administration sought to complete the campaign initiated by neoliberals and fully dismantle faculty power. The Trump administration has deprofessionalized education as an academic discipline by restricting its eligibility for federal student loans, thereby rendering it a less attractive and less influential profession.[30] Academic freedom, already weakened during the neoliberal era, has been effectively eradicated for many faculty members during Trump's second term. For example, in Oklahoma, an instructor was removed following a grading dispute amplified by Turning Point USA; in Texas, a student's viral recording of a lesson on gender identity led to a firing; and in Indiana, a professor faced a formal complaint simply for discussing personal politics.[31] Such cases are facilitated by the surveillance mechanisms of Big Tech in the classroom, a practice normalized under neoliberalism. This surveillance is increasingly codified by law, with states like Ohio and Florida requiring searchable databases of course outlines to invite public scrutiny.[32] Relatedly, Trump's allies in various states are delivering a final blow to a tenure system already weakened by the neoliberal era. By freezing tenure-track hiring and implementing 'reforms' aimed at its total abolition, they are systematically dismantling faculty job security.[33]

Trump's push for ideological homogeneity on college campuses sought to quell criticisms of Israel. A large contingent of Trump's base was supportive of Israel and the campus crackdown on Gaza encampments. Indeed, figures such as Christopher Rufo framed Trump's demonization of "wokeness" as part of a broader war on rising antisemitism, which he blamed on DEI policies.[34] To appease this part of the MAGA coalition, Trump targeted students, faculty, and institutions under the auspices of combatting antisemitism.[35] As a result, international students such as Mohsen Mahdawi of Columbia University were detained and Momodou Taal at Cornell University had a visa revoked due to their pro-Palestinian activism.[36] Similarly, Tufts University student Rümeysa Öztürk was detained by six plainclothes Department of Homeland Security (DHS) agents and imprisoned for 45 days, following a visa revocation because of an op-ed she wrote that was sympathetic to the plight of Palestinians.[37] Federal agents detained Columbia University student Mahmoud Khalil without a warrant and attempted to revoke his visa, despite his lawful permanent residency, because he served as a principled negotiator between the Gaza solidarity encampments and the university. Yet the government's justification for his 104-day imprisonment, while his pregnant wife gave birth, did not rest on criminal charges but on a Cold War–era provision that allows deportation if a foreign national's presence threatens U.S. foreign policy interests.[38] An international scholar in legal standing at Georgetown, Badar Khan Suri, was detained for allegedly promoting antisemitism and Hamas propaganda.[39]

The promotion of ideological homogeneity through force under the auspices of combatting hate intensified after the September 2025 assassination of Charlie Kirk. Kirk was fatally shot during a college campus event in Utah; while the motives remain under investigation, conservatives quickly framed the killing as evidence of leftist hostility toward free speech. Using this narrative, Trump signed an executive order targeting individuals accused of "anti-Americanism, anti-capitalism, and anti-Christianity; support for the overthrow of the United States Government; extremism on migration, race, and gender; and hostility towards those who hold traditional American views on family, religion, and morality."[40] This effectively justified broad punitive actions against dissenters. Universities and school districts scrambled to look tough on Kirk's critics to avoid threats of funding cuts. Within days, more than forty faculty, staff, and students across universities were suspended, disciplined, or fired for comments deemed disrespectful of Kirk or for expressing critical reflections on gun violence and unequal responses to shootings.[41] For example, in a clear violation of academic freedom, which protects faculty from retribution for expressing ideas both on and off campus, a college professor in North Carolina was fired for a social media post. Regarding Kirk, the professor wrote: "Did he deserve to die? No. But he was a racist piece of shit. And Turning Point USA is a racist, piece-of-shit organization."[42] Students posting irreverent commentary were expelled and, in several high-profile cases, arrested.[43]

Governing the MAGAcademy

In addition to attacks, Trump also relied on coercion to reshape education in MAGA's image. Federal funding became a blunt instrument of coercion. Billions in research grants and contracts were threatened or frozen unless universities complied with extreme ideological demands, including dismantling DEI programs, auditing foreign funding, enforcing definitions of antisemitism, and altering admissions and hiring policies.[44] In order to receive federal funding, universities would have to make concessions such as reducing the number of international students, eradicating DEI programs and gender-neutral facilities, and submitting to investigations of antisemitism, racial discrimination, and admissions practices.[45] Some accepted agreements, but the capitulation often resulted in more demands from the Trump Administration.[46] By December 2025 universities across the nation reported massive job and program cuts due to the changing budget.[47]

As far as conservatives were concerned, the most prized institution for dismantling was the DOE. Although the first Department of Education was established in 1867, it was almost immediately stripped of its departmental status. Facing intense political pushback, it was downgraded to an office within the Department of the Interior, where it remained for decades.[48] Since its re-establishment as a cabinet-level department under President Jimmy Carter in 1979, the DOE has faced a persistent conservative campaign for its total eradication.[49] Carter created the department to elevate education as a national priority, streamline federal funding, and enforce civil rights, transferring responsibilities previously housed within the Department of Health, Education, and Welfare. From President Ronald Reagan onward, Republican leaders positioned the DOE as a symbol of federal overreach, even when their negative predictions failed to materialize. Trump was no exception. He argued that the DOE was inefficient and lacked accountability and thus had to be dismantled.[50] He said "I'd like it to be closed immediately. The Department of Education's a big con job," and referred to it as "ineffective, wasteful and dominated by radical leftists."[51]

While much of what the DOE does focuses on K–12 education, it also handles major higher education functions. The DOE is responsible for managing federal student loans for 44 million Americans by originating them, servicing the loan portfolios, processing applications for aid and repayment plans, and collecting on defaulted loans.[52] Relatedly, the DOE also handles Pell Grants, a federal financial aid program for undergraduate students with exceptional financial need. It also provides federal oversight by working with the Civil Rights Office to ensure civil rights enforcement in higher education. In addition, the DOE funds significant research in higher education, primarily through its Office of Science, which supports academic institutions in fields including energy, climate, and fundamental science.[53] This funding is directed towards projects, user facilities, and development of the scientific workforce. The DOE also plays a role in higher education research by sponsoring studies, collecting data, and supporting programs such as the Education Innovation and Research (EIR) Program to improve educational practices and policies.

On March 20, 2025, Trump signed an executive order instructing Education Secretary Linda McMahon, herself from the corporate world of pro-wrestling entertainment, to shrink and restructure the department.[54] Although the DOE cannot be abolished without congressional approval, McMahon initiated mass layoffs, cutting nearly half the staff, including employees in the Office for Civil Rights and teams responsible for communications, legal work, and financial aid. In practice, the DOE's core functions were transferred to other federal agencies, leaving the DOE intact in name only.[55] Programs supporting students with disabilities, teacher preparation, and essential research infrastructure were suspended or eliminated. These actions were justified as necessary to reduce waste, even though they undermined the very services the department was designed to provide. Echoing neoliberals' fetish for efficiency, the administration insisted this fragmentation would streamline operations.

The Algorithmic Lobotomy

Trump's second term was bolstered by a symbiotic alliance with the ultra-wealthy, particularly influential figures within the Big Tech sector. Historically, wealthy capitalists viewed democratic governance as a hindrance to their power and accumulation of wealth. It is therefore unsurprising that Trump built upon neoliberal precedents to further privatize higher education, reducing the influence of the electorate while consolidating control in the hands of the private sector. For example, Trump signed an executive order aimed at promoting more corporate partnerships with Historically Black Colleges and Universities (HBCUs), rather than direct government assistance.[56] Similarly, he proposed off-loading the federal student loan portfolio, valued at approximately $1.7 trillion, to private investors.[57] Critics, including Senators Elizabeth Warren and Bernie Sanders, have condemned this move as a "giveaway to wealthy insiders" that would harm working-class students and taxpayers alike.[58]

Trump also signaled that he was going to let the market dictate education and research. For instance, Trump's budget cuts to the National Institutes of Health (NIH) severely disrupted hundreds of vital clinical trials in infectious diseases, cancer, and cardiovascular research, undermining public health innovation and federal research capacity.[59] These cuts represent more than a withdrawal of public investment in essential science; they signal a deliberate shift in responsibility toward the private sector. By eroding public research in health and science, the administration ensures that future breakthroughs are subject to the whims of corporate funding, prioritizing profit margins over equitable public benefit. This market-driven logic extends to student aid. Under a restructured federal framework, the government no longer recognizes disciplines such as nursing, social work, education, and architecture as professional degrees.[60] By restricting loan access for these service-oriented fields while expanding it for those favored by the private market, the administration is effectively incentivizes students to calibrate their education toward market demand rather than democratic necessity.

Trump's education agenda further serves private industry by facilitating massive giveaways to his allies in Big Tech. In 2025, a coalition of tech titans, ranging from Peter Thiel (PayPal, Palantir) and Elon Musk (X, Tesla) to Mark Zuckerberg (Meta), rallied behind the administration.[61] Consequently, it is no surprise that Trump's educational framework mirrors the neoliberal "techno-fetishism" that once tethered these donors to the Democratic Party. Most notably, Trump has staked his administration's legitimacy on the promise of Artificial Intelligence, punctuated by an executive order barring states from regulating the industry.[62] In addition, Trump has utilized executive orders to mandate the integration of AI education throughout the national school system. Most notably, in April 2025, President Trump signed the Executive Order "Advancing Artificial Intelligence Education for American Youth." The order establishes a national framework to bolster AI literacy and proficiency by integrating AI into standard curricula, providing comprehensive technical training for educators, and fostering early student exposure to emerging technologies. These initiatives are designed to cultivate an "AI-ready" workforce and secure the next generation of American innovators.[63]

Trump's AI education policies mirror the rhetoric of industry boosters, largely ignoring the negative impacts of technology on learning while casting AI as an inevitable, transformative force. This framework suggests that institutions must embrace AI to survive the pressures of a competitive global economy.[64] This mirrors the neoliberal justifications used thirty years ago to argue for the mass introduction of digital tools in the classroom. However, decades later, research reveals a troubling trend: Gen Z is the first generation to demonstrate a decline in cognitive skills. Neuroscientist Jared Cooney Horvath points out that while standardized tests may not measure innate intelligence, they do track cognitive skills;

consequently, Gen Z is "the first generation in modern history to score lower on standardized tests than the previous one."[65] Horvath cites examples like Maine, which launched an aggressive $50 million initiative over two decades ago to put laptops in schools but saw no subsequent improvement in student achievement. He warns that early research on AI portends a similar negative outcome on learning.[66] Despite this, the Trump administration continues to push Big Tech into the classroom, treating AI as a "neoliberal fetish" regardless of the cognitive risks.

Through public-private partnerships, grant prioritization, and national competitions targeting K–12 exposure, teacher training, and apprenticeships, Trump's AI policy positions education primarily as a pipeline for industry, reducing it to skill acquisition and workforce preparation. Students are urged to become "AI innovators" rather than critical thinkers or engaged democratic citizens, and teachers are expected to undergo retraining to incorporate AI into classrooms and instructional design.[67] The establishment of an Artificial Intelligence Education Task Force composed of federal agencies and industry-aligned policymakers underscores a belief that technological development should be coordinated by government, corporations, and philanthropy, sidelining educators and communities.[68] Illustrating how far collective bargaining units had drifted in the neoliberal era from representing workers in opposition to corporations, the American Federation of Teachers (AFT), led by President Randi Weingarten, followed the lead of the Trump administration and signed a $23 million AI training initiative for its members, funded by major tech companies including OpenAI, Microsoft, and Anthropic.[69]

While AI has existed for seventy years, recent advancements in high-speed computing have merely perfected the illusion of intelligence.[70] As scholars consistently observe, current iterations of AI are not truly "intelligent." At best, they execute menial tasks with rigid obedience; at worst, they fail to navigate complex, real-world variables.[71] For instance, an AI-managed vending machine that, unable to adapt to simple manipulation, began dispensing items for free.[72] More alarming is the pseudo-objectivity of these systems. AI reflects the inherent biases of its creators and the data sets used for training.[73] This was starkly demonstrated when Elon Musk's GrokAI bot disseminated White Supremacist conspiracies, including the "white genocide" myth in South Africa, and even referred to itself as "Mecha Hitler."[74] Lacking a moral compass, AI has also been implicated in aiding teen suicide and facilitating the expansion of child pornography.[75]

The practical utility of AI is equally questionable. One study found that AI-generated news summaries were inaccurate 45 percent of the time.[76] Other studies have found AI fabricating information from 66 percent to over 88 percent of the time.[77] Similarly, when *The Washington Post* implemented AI to generate customized podcasts, research revealed the content was rife with fabrications, further entrenching users in error-filled confirmation bubbles.[78] These "hallucinations," the fabrication of facts, have already resulted in professional ruin, as evidenced by the lawyer who lost his license after submitting a brief filled with fake case law, or the education ethics committee that discovered its AI-drafted report was based on non-existent studies.[79]

The inherent shortcomings of so-called AI led philosopher Michael Clune to describe the integration of these technologies into higher education as institutions "preparing to self-lobotomize."[80] Indeed, a growing body of research reveals AI's profound limitations and threats to learning. Research indicates that prolonged AI use may negatively alter cognitive functions, specifically impairing the ability to retain basic facts and maintain deep reading comprehension.[81] Furthermore, there is a growing concern that over-reliance on AI in educational settings stifles the development of essential skills, namely critical thinking, complex problem-solving, and original thought.[82] Beyond individual cognitive impacts, surveys suggest that the integration of AI often comes at the expense of vital peer-to-peer and student-teacher relationships.[83] This shift is driven, in part, by a moral panic regarding AI's impact on learning. Faculty now face intense pressure, stemming from professional obligation as well as expectations from peers and administration, to act as a police force tasked with catching cheaters. This adversarial role erodes the foundation of trust essential for effective pedagogy. Consequently, educators are trapped in a grueling dilemma: exhausting themselves hunting for AI usage or radically redesigning their entire curricula to mitigate the risk of dishonesty.

Despite these concerns, educational institutions are leaning further into corporate partnerships. For example, the California State University (CSU) system, the nation's largest public university with nearly half a million students, recently announced a $17 million deal with OpenAI, the creator of ChatGPT. This massive investment in "Big Tech" occurred even as the CSU system was simultaneously cutting faculty and staff positions across its 23 campuses. Ronald Purser, a Research Professor of Management at San Francisco State University, summed it up: "Students use AI to write papers, professors use AI to grade them, degrees become meaningless, and tech companies make fortunes. Welcome to the death of higher education."[84]

A New Civic Resistance?

The resistance to MAGAcademy policies in higher education has been slow, but growing, over the first year of Trump's second term. At first, many higher education institutions capitulated. The University of Pennsylvania removed transgender athletes from its records; Columbia University overhauled admissions, policing, and academic programs; University of California, Berkeley shared 160 names of students and faculty investigated for alleged antisemitic incidents; and Brown University adopted the administration's biological definitions of gender and halted gender-affirming care for minors.[85]

Initially, many of these remained process-oriented neoliberal institutions, believing that strict adherence to process and a focus on the bottom line would ensure their success. However, two things changed. First, schools noticed how badly the reputation of institutions such as Columbia had been battered by giving into Trump. When Columbia signed a deal adhering to Trump's demands, Claire Shipman, Columbia's acting president, sold it as a deal that "safeguards our independence."[86] However, critics disagreed, arguing that Columbia had effectively lost its intellectual independence to the Trump administration. Furthermore, the university dropped two spots in the prestigious U.S. News & World Report Best National Universities rankings for 2026, falling to 15th, the lowest of the prestigious Ivy League schools. This combination of bad publicity and declining rankings is precisely the kind of outcome that alarms the image-obsessed professional managerial class (PMC).[87]

Second, it became clear that Trump would not stop until he received pushback. In October, he proposed "The Trump Higher Education Compact" to nine universities, which tied funding to the schools' providing feedback that they are adhering to the administration's priorities.[88] The reality was that years of austerity had left most universities dependent on annual federal funding. Wealthier institutions like Massachusetts Institute of Technology, Dartmouth College, and the University of Pennsylvania, did not need the Compact, but others did.[89] Institutions like Vanderbilt and Arizona State University agreed to provide feedback as required by the Compact, and the University of Texas, Austin initially considered doing the same.[90] Others postured resistance but then capitulated, such as the University of Virginia, which publicly rejected the Compact, then privately negotiated its own deal to end federal investigations into admissions and hiring. It accepted a DOJ mandate, avoided a monetary penalty, and quietly internalized the administration's racial framework, sidestepping the spectacle of formally joining the Compact.[91] Similarly, Brown University rejected the Compact because its president, Christina Paxson, insisted the arrangement would undermine governance autonomy, even as the university had quietly entered a separate federal agreement months earlier.[92]

Outside of the PMC, academic organizations and collective bargaining units provided some of the resistance. Organizations like the American Association of University Professors (AAUP) and AFT largely relied on legal and grassroots strategies.[93] They filed lawsuits to challenge the administration's policies, defend immigrant scholars, and reverse punitive funding cuts, while organizing campus rallies and national days of action. According to a November 2025 report from *The Guardian*, student, faculty, and staff protests had expanded significantly, with coordinated actions on more than 100 campuses nationwide. These actions reflected a deepening and broadening movement, with leaders like AAUP President Todd Wolfson emphasizing the need for students, faculty, and staff to unite as a "new political force" to defend higher education and democracy itself.[94]

The judiciary has provided a necessary check where executive university leadership has faltered. For example, the University of California, Los Angeles (UCLA) was targeted with a $1.2 billion fine by the Trump administration's Department of Justice (DOJ). The administration alleged violations of Title VI of the Civil Rights Act, claiming the university failed to protect Jewish and Israeli students, used race as an admissions criterion, and recognized transgender students' gender identities.[95] Subsequent reporting, however, revealed that DOJ lawyers were pressured to "find" evidence that the university had illegally tolerated antisemitism. This fabrication proved too much for several officials, who resigned and denounced the investigations as "fraudulent."[96] While UCLA's executive leadership initially agreed to cooperate and entered negotiations with the administration, faculty from UC San Francisco, UC Berkeley, and eventually UCLA joined a countersuit.[97] Upon review, a federal judge blocked the administration from withholding funds, citing the DOJ's coercive tactics.[98] In February 2026, the Trump administration officially dropped its appeal of the injunction.[99]

Conclusion

For those who oppose the MAGAcademy, the acts of resistance shine as rare beacons of hope in the dark landscape of higher education. They spark a contagious spirit of action rooted in a deep commitment to learning, knowledge, and freedom. Yet, there is a real danger in falling into a familiar trap of America's divided political arena: treating Trump or MAGA as the problem itself rather than the symptom of a deeper, systemic disease wrought by the two-party system.

Trump will one day disappear from the public stage, but the MAGAcademy and the impulses that contributed to its rise will remain. When that day comes, it would be a grave mistake to simply return to the neoliberal status quo, where the corporatization of higher education is normalized, faculty are reduced to contingent labor, and students are seen merely as paying customers. The way students and faculty are treated, the overwhelming power imbalances on campuses, and the funding models that dictate priorities all must be fundamentally transformed, and quickly, if the pursuit of happiness and the very health of democracy still matter to the people of this nation. The next chapter will explore bold alternatives and necessary correctives to the MAGAcademy and the devastation neoliberalism has inflicted on higher education.

6

Dismantling the MAGAcademy

Bulldozers rolled into the White House grounds in the fall of 2025 to begin constructing a 90,000-square-foot ballroom over the East Wing. Originally priced at $200 million, the project's cost surged to $400 million within months.[1] This structure, promised for completion by the end of President Donald Trump's second term in 2029, will stand as a monument to excess, nearly twice the size of the original White House itself.[2] By replacing the historic East Wing with a sprawling venue funded by the giants of the Professional Managerial Class (PMC), the building functions as a physical manifestation of corporate capture. Indeed, the contributors to the project include some of the wealthiest corporations and people in the world, from Amazon, Google, and Palantir to billionaire families such as the Lutnicks and Winklevosses.[3]

This transformation of the White House offers a vivid symbol of what decades of neoliberal marketization have produced. Neoliberalism suggests human well-being is best advanced by enabling individual entrepreneurial freedoms within a framework characterized by strong private property rights and free markets. Anyone who visited Washington, D.C., before this turn would remember that the public employees of the richest nation on earth worked in worn, unimpressive buildings. Their modesty served as a reminder that government was a public service. Today, private corporations and well-paid lobbyists have moved so far into the corridors of power that they are literally reshaping the "People's House."

The central crisis of our time is that this corporate expansion coincided with the measurable decline of American democracy. The Economist Intelligence Unit (EIU), a global organization that tracks the health of political systems, documented the United States shifting from a "full democracy" in 2007 to a "flawed democracy" by 2025.[4] This decline stems from the inherent contradiction between democracy, which depends on collective decision-making, and capitalism, which elevates individual self-interest. The physical reshaping of the White House mirrors the internal reshaping of the nation's civic soul.

The White House was not the only institution consumed; public education was, too. Neoliberals promised that treating higher education like a corporation would make it more efficient and innovative. Yet, as the university adopted corporate logic, democracy withered and the MAGAcademy emerged. During the neoliberal era, poverty reached historic highs, and wealth inequality became the worst it had been since the 1920s.[5] Child poverty tripled between 2021 and 2024, and by 2023, 37 percent of adults could not cover a $400 emergency expense.[6] Neoliberals insisted that education would fix these problems, but while the percentage of degree holders has tripled since the 1970s, economic instability has only grown worse. Part of reversing the trends that brought about the MAGAcademy will depend on liberating the university from the market-driven hubris of the managerial class. Here are my proposals to reclaim higher education from corporate control and realign it to truly serve the people.

Proposal 1:
Replace Virtue Signaling with Honesty

A consistent theme throughout the neoliberal era is the hubris of the PMC. In the neoliberal era, the government stopped funding critical services such as mental health, housing, and food security. Simultaneously, it balked at addressing the healthcare crisis or the epidemic of gun violence. The PMC responded with a "shoestring" fantasy: it claimed higher education could solve these massive societal failures if it were simply managed more aggressively.

This approach must be abandoned. While higher education is a powerful tool, it cannot be a substitute for a functioning social safety net. The PMC skirts accountability by putting these social problems front and center in university rhetoric but offering corporate solutions that fail to address the root causes while exacerbating the financial strain on the institution. This is "virtue signaling," action based on feelings and branding rather than evidence, which only makes the public more skeptical of the university's utility. We must distinguish what a college can realistically do and demand the government use other structures and resources to address the rest.

Higher education has become a "catch-all" blamed for every failure of the American state. When we ask a university to solve the housing crisis or the mental health epidemic, we are essentially asking a school to act as a Department of Health and Human Services. This is the definition of mission creep, the gradual expansion of an organization's goals beyond its original purpose.

We must demand that the federal government establish or empower dedicated agencies to handle these non-educational crises. For example: The Department of Housing and Urban Development (HUD) should manage student and community housing initiatives directly, removing the burden from university budgets. The Department of Health and Human Services (HHS) should be the primary funder and provider of mental health services on and near campuses, integrated with broader public health networks.

Relatedly, given the rise of school shootings during the neoliberal era, educators are now being asked to detect potential shooters and, in some cases, even arm themselves to protect their classrooms.[7] This is a problem the nation as a whole, not just higher education, must confront. As Rita Mae Brown said, "The definition of insanity is doing the same thing over and over again and expecting different results."[8] Schools need to be honest: this is not a challenge they can solve alone. Instead of narrowly blaming the economy, video games, violent movies, mental health, bad parenting, or culture shifts, we must consider all these factors and more. We need to admit that schools cannot fully protect students; security cameras only document who is responsible after the fact. Schools and communities must work together on holistic solutions that are addressed at the local, state, and federal levels, where higher education plays a role but is not the sole solution.

When these services are handled by the state, the university can shed the thousands of professional managerial roles currently dedicated to "overseeing" these crises and hopefully put them in the hands of people who are actually qualified and have resources to address them. This allows for a "lean" administrative structure that serves education.

<h2 style="text-align:center">Proposal 2:
Abandon the "College for All" Mandate</h2>

While higher education is a vital space for personal growth and democratic development, we must stop treating it as a mandatory survival requirement. Forcing attendance on those who are uninterested or unready is a failure to respect diverse life goals. This compulsion harms the students themselves, who spend years in a state of unfulfillment, and it degrades the classroom environment.

When a classroom is populated by students whose only objective is to "pass" as a means to enter corporate life and maximize wealth, the intellectual engagement of the collective suffers. Educators frequently find that these reluctant students consume a disproportionate amount of time. They are often the ones deploying "dead grandma" excuses—the common term for the sudden influx of family emergencies and technical glitches used to justify late work. Meanwhile, students who genuinely seek deeper inquiry are sidelined. When these engaged learners are forced into group projects with peers who are merely checking a box, they lose the opportunity to connect with fellow scholars and conduct a true investigation of the subject.

Simultaneously, we must promote vocational and technical alternatives with the same vigor we have traditionally reserved for higher education. Reinvesting in manual skills, technical training, arts, and on-the-job apprenticeships provides a dignified path for those who do not desire a broad general education. Regardless of the chosen path, the standard of living for these citizens should match that of college graduates. This shift would respect individual choice in a free society and prevent the wealthy from "gaming" the system through expensive admissions coaching and questionable accommodations. Ultimately, the college classroom would return to being a place of scholarship rather than a mandatory obstacle course for employment.

Proposal 3:
Faculty Power: The Mechanics of Collective Action

The restoration of the university depends on faculty solidarity. This is not merely about better pay; it is about shared governance, the principle that faculty should have primary responsibility for the fundamental academic decisions of the institution. Faculty members need to have power so they can assert certain truths, such as the fact that our constitutional rights and freedoms and those of our students need to be protected everywhere, including on campus.

The corporatization of the university has systematically erased faculty power. This happened through adjunctification, the process of replacing stable, tenure-track faculty with part-time, low-paid instructors who have no job security. If higher education is to survive as a democratic institution, we must reverse this trend. Non-tenure-track positions should account for no more than 10 percent of faculty, reserved only for emergencies. The rest must be stable, tenure-track roles.

To achieve this, the faculty, the creators of knowledge, must show a "spine." Those with tenure must strike in solidarity with their graduate students and part-time colleagues to shut down institutions until they are reoriented from the PMC back to the educators. This is a battle for the integrity of the profession, and it rests on three propositions:

1. The 90 percent Rule: Faculty unions must bargain for contracts that mandate 90 percent of all instructional hours be performed by tenure-track professors. This eliminates the "gig economy" model of adjunctification.

2. The Bureaucratic Boycott: Faculty should collectively refuse to participate in "assessment" and "reporting" metrics that serve institutional branding rather than student learning. By "starving" the administrative machine of data, faculty force a return to qualitative academic standards.

3. The Solidarity Strike: Tenure-track faculty must be willing to walk out in support of graduate student researchers and part-time lecturers. Neoliberalism thrives by isolating these groups; solidarity destroys that leverage.

Proposal 4:
Reclaim Pedagogy from the Machine

While technology is often marketed as a panacea for the challenges of modern education, we must remain realistic about its limitations and its unintended consequences. Smart devices and so-called Artificial Intelligence (AI) can, in specific contexts, enhance research or streamline administrative tasks. For example, some schools are using AI to assess admissions essays from prospective students.[9] Mounting evidence suggests that the pervasive integration of these tools often undermines deep learning.[10] The constant presence of "smart" tech has reoriented our neural pathways to be slower and less methodical, favoring rapid information retrieval over the rigorous, critical thinking required for democratic participation. When the classroom is flooded with gadgets, the space for sustained intellectual struggle is often replaced by a distracted, surface-level engagement with data.

The decision to integrate or reject specific technologies must be driven by professional faculty, not by "tech overlords" or the corporate fetishizing PMC. Administrators often have an ideological disposition toward "disruption," the neoliberal belief that market inventions are inherently superior to traditional professional practices. This leads to the forced adoption of expensive platforms and software that serve the interests of Silicon Valley rather than the needs of students. Faculty, as the primary architects of the learning environment, are the only ones qualified to assess whether a tool genuinely improves scholarship or merely serves as a high-tech distraction. Thus, faculty must be listened to and not dismissed as out of touch or old-fashioned when they criticize the harmful effects of technology on their profession. Reclaiming the campus means ensuring that pedagogical evidence, rather than corporate marketing, dictates the presence of technology in the classroom.

Proposal 5:
Embrace Intellectual Diversity

The neoliberal approach to identity politics collapsed in 2024 in part because it rested on racist and sexist assumptions that those of us in higher education must confront and avoid repeating in the future. Much of the neoliberal rhetoric on identity is reductive, assuming that Black people care only about criminal justice reform, Latinos care only about immigration, and women care only about abortion. While many people who share these identities do care about these issues, they also care, like everyone else, about a wide range of concerns, including their material conditions. Reductive thinking such as the neoliberal managerial rhetoric on identity epitomizes prejudice.

If DEI had truly diversified campus ideology to make space for leftists, conservatives, and others, this reductive stereotyping would have been harder to sustain. There would also have been less shock that women, Latinos, Black voters, and young people increased their support for Trump in 2024.[11] People are diverse. As a result, commentators would not make claims such as "this country is not ready for a woman president," especially when a majority of voters supported a female candidate, Hillary Clinton, in the 2016 election.[12]

Higher education must make space for truly oppositional views, including Marxism (the study of class struggle and the critique of capitalism) and conservatism (the preference for traditional institutions and limited government). This does not mean including ideologies that are antagonistic toward the scholarly process of discovering knowledge such as fascism, an authoritarian, ultranationalist political ideology characterized by dictatorial power and the suppression of opposition. Instead, it means making space for critical educators who question power and dominant ideologies, including those institutionalized by the university itself. By focusing on intellectual diversity rather than demographic branding, the university can reclaim its role as a place of honest inquiry and can avoid the reductive mistakes that have bastardized identity in contemporary discourses.

Proposal 6:
Build the Civic University

The path forward is found not in nostalgia, but rather in the radical courage to reclaim the public purpose of education. The 2024 election was a rejection of a neoliberal system that gaslit the public and ignored their lived experiences. This frustration was made manifest when the CEO of UnitedHealthcare, Brian Thompson, was shot in New York City; the public's widespread sympathy for the suspect, Luigi Mangione, revealed a deep-seated anger toward the corporate policies the neoliberal era defended.[13]

To move beyond the neoliberal ruin, we must rebuild the "Civic University," an institution that prioritizes its role as a democratic anchor over its identity as a corporate brand.[14] At the heart of this reconstruction is the cultivation of social capital, the networks, norms, and trust that enable participants to act together more effectively to pursue shared objectives. For decades, the university has operated as an extraction machine, pulling tuition from families and labor from precarious faculty while offering little back to the surrounding community but "town-gown" tension and gentrification. A true civic university rejects this isolation, choosing instead to become an institution that fosters the intangible bonds of reciprocity that hold a democracy together.

The urgency of this task is best understood through the lens of Robert Putnam's seminal work, *Bowling Alone: The Collapse and Revival of American Community*.[15] Putnam argues that American democracy is in peril because our "social capital" has plummeted; we no longer join clubs, trust our neighbors, or engage in the face-to-face collective life that makes self-governance possible. When applied to higher education, the neoliberal era has effectively "bowled alone" by transforming students into isolated consumers and campuses into gated enclaves.

To reverse this, the university must proactively restore trust by treating its local area as a partner rather than a laboratory. This means the university must take a lead role in improving regional housing, public safety, and economic stability—not as a "ruler" dictating terms from on high, but as a stakeholder whose own survival depends on the health of its neighbors. And it means meaningful collaboration between communities and campuses, drawing on John Dewey's concept of service learning, in which students connect academic study to real-world problems through active engagement in public and community life.[16] By creating shared spaces and mutual initiatives, the university moves from being a credential factory to becoming a hub of civic revitalization, proving that higher education is not a luxury for the few, but a vital utility for the many.

There is hope in this struggle. By returning power to educators, rejecting the "market commodity" model of learning, and demanding the state take responsibility for social crises, we can ensure that higher education becomes a force for democratic renewal. The task is urgent, the crisis palpable, but the road map is clear. We can choose to be a casualty of this era, or we can choose to be the architects of what comes next.

Proposal 7:
Reject Austerity Propaganda

The most common neoliberal refrain used to block reform is the question "How will we pay for it?" This defense rests on a manufactured sense of scarcity. To reclaim higher education, we must first dismantle the myth of scarcity and expose the "austerity propaganda" that suggests the nation is too poor to educate its own citizens. This defense relies on manufactured scarcity, the political strategy of claiming a lack of funds for public goods while simultaneously approving massive expenditures for corporate interests. It relies on absurd analogies such as "just like a household, we need to manage expenses," ignoring the fact that households don't print money, control global currency, or have armies—but I digress.

For decades, the public has been gaslit into believing that a debt-free education is a fiscal impossibility, yet the true impossibility is sustaining a democracy in which the path to knowledge is gated by predatory lending and stagnant wages. In reality, resources to fund tuition-free public higher education are already present within the economy; they are simply being diverted into corporate subsidies and an ever-expanding administrative bureaucracy.

Accessing funding for tuition-free higher education is not a matter of creating new wealth, but of aggressively reclaiming public resources that have been diverted into private hoards and administrative excess. They are rechanneled into the hands of the wealthy through tax loopholes and corporate subsidies. During the neoliberal era, the top 1 percent of Americans captured an estimated $50 trillion from the bottom 90 percent.[17] By 2025, the top 10 percent of U.S. households accounted for nearly half of all consumer spending.[18] The money is available. Reclaiming it requires targeted tax reforms that confront the extreme concentration of wealth produced by decades of neoliberal policy.

If neoliberals demand budget cuts, they should start with administrative bloat. If they wish to generate revenue, they should tax the wealthy. To achieve this, the public must be led to reject the rhetoric that the wealthy are "job creators." As the Department of Justice files related to the late financier and sex offender Jeffrey Epstein suggest, the ultra-wealthy are often not titans of industry, but a cohort of tax dodgers, sex criminals, insider traders, and corrupt individuals who have infiltrated law, media, politics, entertainment, and technology. They are not the engines of our economy; they are the beneficiaries of a runaway system of corruption.[19] To reclaim these funds, we must embrace a financial blueprint that targets the extreme concentration of wealth produced by the neoliberal era. For instance, the so-called One Big Beautiful Bill Act (OBBBA) of 2025, despite its complex introduction of "Trump Accounts" and the expansion of 529 plans (tax-advantaged savings accounts designed to encourage saving for future education costs), inadvertently highlighted the massive, untapped potential of excise taxes. An excise tax is a legislated tax imposed on specific goods or services at the time of purchase or on specific income. Currently, only a small fraction of multibillion-dollar private university endowments are taxed.[20] Increasing the excise tax on investment income for institutions with endowments exceeding a certain threshold per student would generate billions in public revenue.[21] Furthermore, a wealth tax, a levy on the total value of personal assets held by the ultra-wealthy, could be earmarked specifically for a federal-state partnership. Under this model, the federal government would match state investments in higher education, provided states eliminate tuition at all public institutions. This is not "new" money; it is the reclamation of public wealth that was privatized over the last forty years. By rejecting the propaganda of austerity, we can restore the university to its rightful place as a fully funded public utility.

Conclusion:
Beyond the Ballroom

The $400 million ballroom in the White House is a hollow monument to a nation that has traded its civic soul for private luxury. It is a physical symbol of how higher education, once the pride and promise of the U.S., became the MAGAcademy. But just as the bulldozers tearing up the White House lawn do not have to be the final word on the American experiment, the MAGAcademy does not have to be the last chapter in higher education. While the neoliberal era engendered a world of profound precarity, it also exposed exactly where our systems are most vulnerable.

I started this book with my meeting with Farley. At the time, it felt like I was witnessing the end of higher education itself. Today, I see it differently: we are witnessing the end of the *neoliberal era* of higher education. The fundamental pillars of our craft—learning, critical thinking, knowledge production, and experimentation—remain more crucially important than ever. Similarly, the ideals of diversity, equity, and inclusion, when pursued as genuine policy rather than vapid corporate rhetoric, remain both aspirational and necessary.

Higher education has never been perfect, but we would be immeasurably poorer –socially, intellectually, and economically, if it ceased to exist. The question, then, is not whether it should exist, but in what form. It is difficult to defend the hollow, anti-rights corporate model that has defined the last few decades, and we must recognize that the MAGAcademy does not seek to reverse those trends. Instead, it has merely exploited the tools and rhetoric of the neoliberal era to exacerbate its worst instincts.

Ultimately, a single party or candidate is not the answer. The people are, and always have been, the answer. This is the beautiful, heavy burden of a government of, by, and for the people: when the system fails, we have only ourselves to blame, but we also have only ourselves to look to for change. Whether "Team Blue" or "Team Red," the public is rightfully angry at the current trajectory of our nation and its universities.

Let us stop repeating the mistakes of the past. Let us stop treating our intellect as a commodity and our students as customers. It is time to reclaim higher education for ourselves and for future generations who deserve its benefits. By reclaiming the university as a public good, narrowing its mission to the relentless pursuit of truth, and empowering the students, educators, and community that make that pursuit possible, we do more than fix a school system. We rebuild the Civic University—an institution that doesn't just grant degrees but creates citizens capable of sustaining a democracy.

Acknowledgments

Authoring a book that criticizes higher education can often feel like an exercise in cynicism; however, my own experience has been far more nuanced. While this work addresses systemic failures and the frequent abuse of power in higher education, it is equally a tribute to the incredible individuals who make the academy worth fighting for. I have been profoundly fortunate to collaborate with people who challenged my assumptions, honed my craft, and showed me what it means to be a better academic, teacher, and human being.

I must start by thanking my students. You make teaching and mentorship the greatest job imaginable. Being surrounded by your energy, curiosity, and brilliance reminds me every day why the future is worth getting excited about. Your humor and your resilience are gifts; keep leaning into them. The world is waiting for what you'll do next.

I owe the very existence of my career to a group of leaders who did more than just manage; they bent over backward to create space for me to explore and develop. I am deeply grateful for the opportunities and respect afforded to me by Elizabeth Abrams, Graham Benton, George Bunch, Mary Cardaras, Mickey Huff, Linda Ivey, Cynthia Lewis, Aims McGuiness, Stuart McElderry, Sara Parker, Lisa Ratchford-Smiley, Ellen Rigsby, Aaron Sachowitz, and Obed Vasquez.

I am lucky to collaborate with a community of scholars who pushed me to improve my craft and shared their vast expertise across a staggering array of subjects. My sincere thanks to Jacob Adams, Ray Baker, Kate Bell, Melissa Cervantes, John Cobrally, Jessica Dubreuil, Daniel Fister, Samantha Francois, John Freytag, Katherine Graham, Mary Ann Irwin, Katrina Keating, Grant Kein, John Kropf,

Chenjerai Kumanyika, Amanda Lashaw, Marcelle Levine, Jen Lyons, Scott Macdougall, Nancy Martinson, Gary Moser, Sanghamitra Niyogi, Sarah-Hope Parmeter, Susan Parkinson, Felicia Perez, Albert Ponce, John Rosen, Donna Smith, Greg Tilis, Andrew Wise, Cindy Wong, and Sherri Yeager.

Often overlooked and under-respected, the staff are the true backbone of academic institutions. We all depend on their labor and brilliance daily. A special, heartfelt shout-out to the late Valerie Ball, whom we lost far too soon, as well as to Lori Erokan, Kendall Harcourt, Lisa Martin, Danuta Sawka, Ashton Theimer, Wanda Washington, and Allyson Wright.

Over the years, I have developed an insightful crew of collaborators. I am lucky to learn from this brilliant group of thinkers and friends: James Preston Allen, Robin Andersen, Katie Arosteguy, Adam Armstrong, Derede Arthur, Jorge Ayala, Nicholas Baham III, Frank Baker, Barry Bookin, Ben Boyington, Aimee Burk, Allison Butler, Robert Carley, Natasha Casey, Vera Chang, Christina Ceisel, Randol Contreras, Dickey, Janice Domingo, Brian Dolber, Elizaveta Friesem, Yonty Friesem, Lorna Garano, Stephen Gennaro, Gordon Glover, Trevor Griffey, Forrest Hartman, Kim Hawkins, Reagan Haynie, Aaron Heresco, Amalia Herrmann, Michael Hoechsmann, Mickey Huff, Brian Karem, Andrew Kennis, Dorothy Kidd, Joseph Klett, Dylan Lazaga, Andy Lee Roth, Caroline Luce, Steve Macek, Susan Maret, Emil Marmol, Abby Martin, Julian McDougall, Michael Niman, Russell Newman, Peter Phillips, Jeb Purucker, Jessica Samuels, Josh Scheer, Robert Scheer, William Schloetel, Max Schmeder, TM Scruggs, Kajal Shahali, Jeff Share, Emily Sinclair, Sydney Sullivan, Andrew T. Tonkovich, Alison Trope, Pieter Van der Vorst, Shealeigh Voitl, Rob Williams, Renee Thomas-Wood, Bill Yousman, Lori Yousman, and Mark Zaid.

A huge shout-out to Mickey Huff, Elizabeth Bell, Henry Giroux, and Robin Andersen; their patience and expertise were essential in making this project a reality. Special thanks are due to Mischa Geracoulis for her expert guidance through the editorial stage, Library of Congress filing, interviews, and panels. Her leadership was truly invaluable, particularly as she balanced an incredibly demanding schedule. Thank you, Mischa! Lastly, I want to express my deep appreciation to Allison Butler, Sydney Sullivan, and Anastasia Berg for their diligent editing of this manuscript at the 11th hour.

I must thank my teachers. A big shout-out to Mr. Langley, Ms. O'Connor, Ms. Thomas, Ms. Davis, Kathryn Olmsted, Paul Sasse, Mickey Huff, and Clarence Walker for starting me on this path. My gratitude also goes to my graduate instructors who shaped my intellectual foundation: Jamal Cooks, Paula Devos, Andrea Goldfien, David Hemphill, Barbara Henderson, Thomas Passananti, and Andrew Wiese. I am also grateful to James Busby and Pat Switzer for the initial push to go to college.

To my family: thank you for everything. To my mom, for your endless patience in getting me through the school system, and to my sister, Danielle, for showing me what it looks like to learn. To my father, for showing me that the working class often understands government and politics far better than credentialed elites. To my educator friends, Monet Diaz-Huth, Dana Jarrett, and Phill and Jen Endicott, thank you for the space to commiserate and the reminders of why this profession matters.

To the "kiddos," from the McGarry, Jarrett, Dudley, and McDaniel families, thank you for reminding me of the pure joy of discovery.

And to the village that encouraged me along the way: Anastasia Berg, Patrick and Patricia Cannon, Jess and Dan Dudley, Andrew Holden, Chris Jarrett, Mickey Huff, Meg Huff, Darren McClane, Andy Loebenstein, Micah Wood, Katie McDaniel, Ray McDaniel (we love ya, brother), and the Lopez, McGarry, Higdon, and Cannon families,

To the subscribers of the *Gaslight Gazette* and *Disinfo Detox*: Thank you for proving that there is a resolute audience that still cares about truth and the discovery of knowledge. Your comments and interactions have helped shape this content and offer hope that there is a large, vibrant community envisioning a better world.

Last, but certainly not least, I must thank my partner-in-crime, wife, and fellow academic, Kacey VanderVorst. Her encouragement and support make everything possible. Without her witty takes on the many absurdities of higher education, this book would lack its heart. Finally, a nod to Vangl and Emma Goldman, the two "bad-ass" dogs who complete our family. It is the coolest family in the world, and I am deeply thankful.

Select Bibliography

AAUP (American Association of University Professors). 1915. "Appendix I: 1915 Declaration of Principles on Academic Freedom and Academic Tenure." Accessed December 11, 2025. https://www.aaup.org/NR/rdonlyres/A6520A9D-0A9A-47B3-B550-C006B5B224E7/0/1915Declaration.pdf.

———. 1940. "1940 Statement of Principles on Academic Freedom and Tenure with 1970 Interpretive Comments." Accessed December 11, 2025. https://www.aaup.org/sites/default/files/1940%20Statement.pdf.

———. 2021. "The Annual Report on the Economic Status of the Profession, 2020–21." https://www.aaup.org/report/annual-report-economic-status-profession-2020-21.

ACLU (American Civil Liberties Union). "Know Your Rights." Accessed December 2025. https://www.aclu.org/know-your-rights.

ACLU of Northern California. 2025. "Know Your Rights: Free Speech, Protests & Demonstrations." December 15, 2025. https://www.aclunorcal.org/know-your-rights/free-speech-protests-demonstrations/.

Andersen, Kurt. *Fantasyland: How America Went Haywire: A 500-Year History.* New York: Random House, 2018.

Andersen, Robin. *The Complicit Lens: US Media Coverage of Israel's Genocide in Gaza.* New York: OR Books, 2026.

Archibald, Robert B., and David H. Feldman. 2011. *Why Does College Cost So Much?* New York: Oxford University Press.

Baker, Bruce D. 2021. *Educational Inequality and School Finance: Why Money Matters for America's Students.* Cambridge, MA: Harvard Education Press.

Baldwin, Davarian L. 2021. *In the Shadow of the Ivory Tower: How Universities Are Plundering Our Cities.* New York: Bold Type Books.

Bartlett, Lora, Alisun Thompson, Judith Warren Little, and Riley Collins. *Going the Distance: The Teaching Profession in a Post-COVID World.* Cambridge, MA: Harvard Education Press, 2024.

Berman, Elizabeth Popp. 2012. *Creating the Market University: How Academic Science Became an Economic Engine.* Princeton, NJ: Princeton University Press.

Blyth, Mark. 2013. *Austerity: The History of a Dangerous Idea.* New York: Oxford University Press.

Bourdieu, Pierre. *Distinction: A Social Critique of the Judgment of Taste.* Translated by Richard Nice. Cambridge, MA: Harvard University Press, 1984.

Broussard, Meredith. *More than a Glitch: Confronting Race, Gender, and Ability Bias in Tech.* Cambridge, MA: MIT Press, 2023.

Childress, Herb. 2019. *The Adjunct Underclass: How America's Colleges Betrayed Their Faculty, Their Students, and Their Mission.* Chicago: University of Chicago Press.

Cowie, Jefferson. 2010. *Stayin' Alive: The 1970s and the Last Days of the Working Class.* New York: The New Press.

Clinton, Hillary Rodham. *What Happened.* New York: Simon & Schuster, 2017.

D'Souza, Dinesh. *Illiberal Education: The Politics of Race and Sex on Campus.* New York: Free Press, 1991.

Davis, John A., and Mark Farrell. *The Market Oriented University: An Inquiry into the Nature of Higher Education Management and Leadership.* Cham: Palgrave Macmillan, 2018.

Delgado, Richard, and Jean Stefancic. *Critical Race Theory: An Introduction.* 3rd ed. New York: New York University Press, 2017.

DiAngelo, Robin. *White Fragility: Why It's So Hard for White People to Talk About Racism.* Boston: Beacon Press, 2018.

deBoer, Fredrik. 2020. *The Cult of Smart: How Our Broken Education System Perpetuates Social Injustice.* New York: St. Martin's Press.

Donen, Tony, Jennifer Anton, Lisa Beard, Todd Stinson, and Glenda Sullivan. *Grades Don't Matter: Using Assessment to Measure True Learning.* New York: Education Press, 2010.

Edmundson, Mark. 2013. *Why Teach?: In Defense Of A Real Education.* New York: Bloomsbury Publishing, 2013.

———. 2018. *The Heart Of The Humanities: Reading, Writing, Teaching.* New York: Bloomsbury.

Ehrenreich, Barbara, and John Ehrenreich. 1977. "The Professional-Managerial Class." *Radical America* 11 (2): 7–20.

Flannery, Teresa. *How to Market a University: Building Value, Creating Visibility, and Inspiring Engagement.* Baltimore: Johns Hopkins University Press, 2021.

Frank, Thomas. *Listen, Liberal: Or, What Ever Happened to the Party of the People?* New York: Metropolitan Books, 2016.

Gerstle, Gary. 2022. *The Rise and Fall of the Neoliberal Order: America and the World in the Free Market Era.* New York: Oxford University Press.

Ginsberg, Benjamin. 2011. *The Fall of the Faculty: The Rise of the All-Administrative University and Why It Matters.* New York: Oxford University Press.

Giroux, Henry A. 2014. *Neoliberalism's War on Higher Education.* Chicago: Haymarket Books.

Givan, Rebecca Kolins, and Amy Schrager Lang, eds. *Strike for the Common Good: Fighting for the Future of Public Education.* Ann Arbor: University of Michigan Press, 2020.

Goddard, Connie. *Learning for Work: How Industrial Education Fostered Democratic Opportunity.* Urbana: University of Illinois Press, 2024.

Goddard, John, Ellen Hazelkorn, and Paul Vallance, eds. *The Civic University: The Policy and Leadership Challenges.* Cheltenham: Edward Elgar Publishing, 2016.

Graeber, David. 2015. *The Utopia of Rules: On Technology, Stupidity, and the Secret Joys of Bureaucracy.* Brooklyn: Melville House.

———. 2019. *Bullshit Jobs: The Rise of Pointless Work, and What We Can Do About It.* London: Penguin.

Gutiérrez y Muhs, Gabriella, Yolanda Flores Niemann, Carmen G. González, and Angela P. Harris, eds. *Presumed Incompetent: The Intersections of Race and Class for Women in Academia.* University Press of Colorado, 2012.

Hacker, Andrew, and Claudia Dreifus. 2010. *Higher Education?: How Colleges Are Wasting Our Money and Failing Our Kids.* New York: Times Books.

Hayes, Thomas. *New Strategies in Higher Education Marketing.* San Francisco, CA: Jossey-Bass, 1991.

Heale, M. J. *McCarthy's Americans: Red Scare Politics in State and Nation, 1935–1965.* London: Macmillan Education UK, 1998.

Higdon, Nolan, and Allison Butler. *Surveillance Education: Navigating the Conspicuous Absence of Privacy in Schools*. New York: Routledge, 2025.

Higdon, Nolan and Mickey Huff. *United States of Distraction: Media Manipulation in Post-Truth America (And What We Can Do About It)*. San Francisco, CA: City Lights Books, 2019.

Horowitz, David. *The Professors: The 101 Most Dangerous Academics in America*. Washington, DC: Regnery Publishing, 2006.

Hughes, Coleman. *The End of Race Politics: Arguments for a Colorblind America*. New York: Thesis, 2024.

Kaufman-Osborn, Timothy V. 2023. *The Autocratic Academy: Reenvisioning Rule within America's Universities*. Durham: Duke University Press.

Klein, Ezra, and Derek Thompson. *Abundance*. New York: Simon and Schuster, 2025.

Lebron, Christopher J. *The Making of Black Lives Matter: A Brief History of an Idea*. Oxford: Oxford University Press, 2017.

Liu, Catherine. 2021. *Virtue Hoarders: The Case Against the Professional Managerial Class*. Minneapolis: University of Minnesota Press.

Lomotey, Kofi, and William A. Smith, eds. *The Racial Crisis in American Higher Education*. Albany, NY: State University of New York Press, 2023.

Mattei, Clara E. 2022. *The Capital Order: How Economists Invented Austerity and Paved the Way to Fascism*. Chicago: University of Chicago Press.

Mazzucato, Mariana. 2013. *The Entrepreneurial State: Debunking Public vs. Private Sector Myths*. London: Anthem Press.

Newfield, Christopher. 2016. *The Great Mistake: How We Wrecked Public Universities and How We Can Fix Them*. Baltimore: Johns Hopkins University Press.

Pincus, Fred L. *Reverse Discrimination: Dismantling the Myth*. Boulder, CO: Lynne Rienner Publishers, 2003.

Putnam, Robert D. *Bowling Alone: The Collapse and Revival of American Community*. New York: Simon and Schuster, 2000.

Rockhill, Gabriel. *Who Paid the Pipers of Western Marxism?* New York: Monthly Review Press, 2025.

Rubio, Philip F. *A History of Affirmative Action, 1619–2000.* Jackson, MS: University Press of Mississippi, 2009.

Quinn, Ryan. 2024. "Faculty Overwhelmingly Back Harris in November. But They Won't Tell Students to Do the Same." *Inside Higher Ed*, October 21, 2024.

Ravitch, Diane. 2010. *The Death and Life of the Great American School System.* New York: Basic Books.

———. 2013. *Reign of Error: The Hoax of the Privatization Movement and the Danger to America's Public Schools.* New York: Alfred A. Knopf.

Schleck, Julia. 2022. *Dirty Knowledge: Academic Freedom in the Age of Neoliberalism.* Lincoln: University of Nebraska Press.

Schuster, Jack H., and Martin J. Finkelstein. *The American Faculty: The Restructuring of Academic Work and Careers.* Baltimore: Johns Hopkins University Press, 2006.

Shermer, Elizabeth Tandy. *Indentured Students: How Government-Guaranteed Loans Left Generations Drowning in College Debt.* Cambridge, MA: Harvard University Press, 2021.

Slaughter, Sheila, and Larry L. Leslie. *Academic Capitalism: Politics, Policies, and the Entrepreneurial University.* Baltimore: Johns Hopkins University Press, 1997.

Sowell, Thomas. *Social Justice Fallacies.* New York: Basic Books, 2023.

Johnson, Andre E., and Amanda Nell Edgar. *The Summer of 2020: George Floyd and the Resurgence of the Black Lives Matter Movement.* Lanham, MD: Lexington Books, 2023.

Taylor, Keeanga-Yamahtta. *From #BlackLivesMatter to Black Liberation.* Chicago: Haymarket Books, 2016.

Thelin, John R. *A History of American Higher Education.* 3rd ed. Baltimore: Johns Hopkins University Press, 2019.

Twenge, Jean M., and W. Keith Campbell. *The Narcissism Epidemic: Living in the Age of Entitlement.* New York: Simon and Schuster, 2009.

Weber, Max. *Economy and Society: A New Translation.* Cambridge, MA: Harvard University Press, 2019 [1921].

Index

Preface

[1] "Fact Sheet: President Donald J. Trump Reforms Accreditation to Strengthen Higher Education," *The White House*, April 23, 2025, www.whitehouse.gov/fact-sheets/2025/04/fact-sheet-president-donald-j-trump-reforms-accreditation-to-strengthen-higher-education; "Restoring Truth and Sanity to American History Executive Orders," *The White House*, March 27, 2025, www.whitehouse.gov/presidential-actions/2025/03/restoring-truth-and-sanity-to-american-history.

Introduction

[1] United States Constitution, Amendment I.

[2] American Civil Liberties Union, "Know Your Rights," www.aclu.org/know-your-rights.

[3] American Civil Liberties Union of Northern California, "Know Your Rights: Free Speech, Protests & Demonstrations," December 15, 2025, www.aclunorcal.org/know-your-rights/free-speech-protests-demonstrations/.

[4] Kery Murakami, "Biden Beats Trump in Higher Ed Contributions," *Inside Higher Ed*, September 11, 2020, www.insidehighered.com/news/2020/09/11/higher-education-workers-gave-five-times-much-biden-trump; Mitchell Langbert and Sean Stevens, "Partisan Registration and Contributions of Faculty in Flagship Colleges," *National Association of Scholars*, January 17, 2020, www.nas.org/blogs/article/partisan-registration-and-contributions-of-faculty-in-flagship-colleges; Ryan Quinn, "Faculty Overwhelmingly Back Harris in November. But They Won't Tell Students to Do the Same," *Inside Higher Ed*, October 21, 2024, www.insidehighered.com/news/faculty-issues/2024/10/21/faculty-heavily-back-harris-they-wont-tell-students.

[5] Gillian Branstetter, "Trump's Executive Orders Promoting Sex Discrimination, Explained," American Civil Liberties Union, January 22, 2025, www.aclu.org/news/lgbtq-rights/trumps-executive-orders-promoting-sex-discrimination-explained; Reuters, "Trump memo asks recipients of federal funds to ban DEI programs," *NBC News*, July 31, 2025, www.nbcnews.com/news/us-news/trump-doj-memo-dei-ban-federal-fund-recipients-rcna222105.

[6] Robin Young and Hafsa Quraishi, "How districts are responding after Trump cleared the way for immigration arrests at schools," *Here & Now* (WBUR/NPR), January 27, 2025, www.npr.org/hereandnow/2025/01/27/immigration-arrests-schools.

[7] Ryan Quinn and Katherine Knott, "$900 Million in Institute of Education Sciences Contracts Axed," *Inside Higher Ed*, February 12, 2025, www.insidehighered.com/news/faculty-issues/research/2025/02/12/900m-institute-education-sciences-contracts-axed; Cory Turner, "The Education Department is being cut in half. Here's what's being lost," *All Things Considered* (NPR), March 13, 2025, www.npr.org/2025/03/12/nx-s1-5325854/trump-education-department-layoffs-civil-rights-student-loans.

[8] Mary Cunningham, "White House asks 9 universities to sign agreement to ensure access to grants and other federal benefits," *CBS News*, October 2, 2025, www.cbsnews.com/news/white-house-nine-universities-compact-federal-funds/.

[9] Karina Tsui, "What we know about the federal detention of activists, students and scholars connected to universities," CNN, updated April 2, 2025, www.cnn.com/2025/03/31/us/what-we-know-college-activists-immigration-hnk; Akela Lacy, "Mohsen Mahdawi Faces Conservative Judges as Trump Administration Tries to Lock Him Back Up," *The Intercept*, September 30, 2025, theintercept.com/2025/09/30/mohsen-mahdawi-ice-detention-trump-columbia/.

[10] Michael Hill, "Cornell Student Protester Facing Deportation Leaves the US on His 'Own Terms'," *Associated Press News*, April 1, 2025, apnews.com/article/cornell-immigration-detention-taal-fc4c3384bd79e0f487d02c85bc023438.

[11] Associated Press, "Tufts student can resume research after Trump officials revoked her visa, judge rules," *The Guardian*, December 9, 2025, www.theguardian.com/us-news/2025/dec/09/rumeysa-ozturk-tufts-student-resume-teaching-visa.

[12] Bianca Quilantan, "'One-sided deal': College presidents see Trump offer rife with peril," *Politico*, October 11, 2025, www.politico.com/news/2025/10/11/academia-resistance-trump-funding-deal-00603781; Alvin Powell, "Harvard won't comply with demands from Trump administration," *Harvard Gazette*, April 14, 2025, news.harvard.edu/gazette/story/2025/04/harvard-wont-comply-with-demands-from-trump-administration/.

[13] "Read the Agreement Between Columbia and the Trump Administration," *The New York Times*, July 24, 2025, www.nytimes.com/interactive/2025/07/24/nyregion/columbia-trump-deal.html; Sam Levin, "UC Berkeley shares 160 names with Trump administration in 'McCarthy era' move," *The Guardian*, September 12, 2025, www.theguardian.com/us-news/2025/sep/12/uc-berkeley-trump-administration-antisemitism.

Chapter One

[1] Gerstle, *The Rise and Fall of the Neoliberal Order;* Mattei, *The Capital Order.*

[2] Blyth, *Austerity.*

[3] Ibid., 109

[4] Fraser and Gerstle, *The Rise and Fall of the New Deal Order, 1930–1980.*

[5] Cowie, *Stayin' Alive*; Schulman, *The Seventies*; Ibid.

[6] Gerstle

[7] Linda Stamato, "The Launch of the Long Game," *Inside Higher Ed,* May 09, 2023, www.insidehighered.com/opinion/views/2023/05/09/powell-memo-helped-launch-attacks-higher-ed-opinion; Jeet Heer, "The Powell Memo Helped Create Project 2025," *The Nation,* September 6, 2024, www.thenation.com/article/society/powell-memo-project-2025-plutocracy/

[8] Gerstle

[9] Mattei

[10] Giroux, *Neoliberalism's War on Higher Education.*

[11] National Commission on Excellence in Education, *A Nation at Risk: The Imperative for Educational Reform* (Washington, DC: U.S. Department of Education, 1983).

[12] Sandia National Laboratories, *The Sandia Report: Perspectives on Education in America* (Albuquerque, NM: U.S. Department of Energy, 1990); Diane Ravitch, *Reign of Error: The Hoax of the Privatization Movement and the Danger to America's Public Schools* (New York: Alfred A. Knopf, 2013); Annie Murphy Paul, "Diane Ravitch Declares the Education Reform Movement Dead," *New York Times*, January 21, 2020.

[13] Giroux.

[14] deBoer, *The Cult of Smart.*

[15] Kohn, *The Case Against Standardized Testing*; Darling-Hammond and Adamson, *Beyond the Bubble Test*; Ravitch, *The Death and Life of the Great American School System*; Ravitch, *Reign of Error.*

[16] Christopher M. Saldaña, "Accountability or Austerity? Examining the Practice of K–12 Early Fiscal Intervention during Periods of Economic Crisis," *Educational Evaluation and Policy Analysis* 47, no. 3 (2025): 907–38.

[17] Jeff Faux, "The Austerity Trap and the Growth Alternative," *World Policy Journal* 5, no. 3
(1988): 367–413.
[18] Corey A. DeAngelis, "Inflation-Adjusted K-12 Education Spending Per Student Has Increased
by 280 Percent Since 1960 on Average, the United States Currently Spends Over $15,000 Per
Student Each Year," *Reason Foundation*, June 15, 2020,
https://reason.org/commentary/inflation-adjusted-k-12-education-spending-per-student-hasincreased-
by-280-percent-since-1960/.
[19] Staff, "How Has Education Funding Changed Over Time?," *Urban Institute*, apps.urban.org/features/education-funding-trends/; Bruce D. Baker and David Knight, "Does Money Matter in Education?," *Albert Shanker Institute* (2025).
[20] Kim Dancy and Rachel Fishman, "More Than Tuition: Higher Education and the Social Safety Net," *New America,* May 24, 2016,
www.newamerica.org/education-policy/edcentral/more-than-tuition-9;
Kelly Field, "Safety Net: Colleges struggle to help their hungry and homeless students," *Chronicle of Higher Education,* February 26, 2017,
www.chronicle.com/article/safety-net
[21] Michael Mitchell, Michael Leachman, and Matt Saenz, "State Higher Education Funding Cuts Have Pushed Costs to Students, Worsened Inequality," *Center on Budget and Policy Priorities,* October 24, 2019,
www.cbpp.org/research/state-budget-and-tax/state-higher-education-funding-cuts-have-pushed-costs-to-students.
[22] Louis Menand, "The Rise and Fall of Neoliberalism The free market used to be touted as the cure for all our problems; now it's taken to be the cause of them," *New Yorker,* July 17, 2023,
www.newyorker.com/magazine/2023/07/24/the-rise-and-fall-of-neoliberalism
[23] Ibid.
[24] Gwen Ifill, "Clinton's Standard Campaign Speech: A Call for Responsibility," *New York Times*, April 26, 1992,
www.nytimes.com/1992/04/26/us/the-1992-campaign-clinton-s-standard-campaign-speech-a-call-for-responsibility.html
[25] Higher Education Amendments of 1992, Pub. L. No. 102-325, 106 Stat. 448 (1992).

26 Sandy Baum, "The Evolution of Student Debt in the U.S.: An Overview" (Washington, DC: Urban Institute, George Washington University Graduate School of Education and Human Development, October 2013); Lyss Welding, "Student Loan Debt Over the Years: 2000s to 2024," *BestColleges*, updated June 27, 2024, www.bestcolleges.com/research/student-loan-debt-by-year/.

27 Melanie Hanson, "Average Student Loan Debt," *EducationData.org*, August 15, 2025, educationdata.org/average-student-loan-debt.

28 Luke Darby, "How Biden Helped Strip Bankruptcy Protection From Millions Just Before a Recession," *GQ*, October 23, 2019, www.gq.com/story/joe-biden-bankruptcy-bill.

29 Kaufman-Osborn, *The Autocratic Academy*.

30 Higdon, "Being on the Outside of the Inside of the Ivory Tower: Nontenured Part-Time Faculty's Attitudes Toward Their Colleagues and Management," *Journal of Education Human*.

31 Ehrenreich and Ehrenreich, "The Professional-Managerial Class," *Radical America*.

32 Liu, *Virtue Hoarders*.

33 FIRE, "The Academic Mind in 2022: What Faculty Think About Free Expression and Academic Freedom on Campus," *The Foundation for Individual Rights and Expression (FIRE)*, www.thefire.org/research-learn/academic-mind-2022-what-faculty-think-about-free-expression-and-academic-freedom.

34 Audrey Wang, "Over 60% of professors identify as liberal, per The Chronicle's faculty survey," *Duke Chronicle,* October 21, 2024, www.dukechronicle.com/article/2024/10/duke-university-faculty-survey-political-leanings-liberal-conservative-moderate-centrist-harvard-yale-variation-across-school-tenure-status-demographics; Meimei Xu, "More than 80 Percent of Surveyed Harvard Faculty Identify as Liberal," *Crimson,* July 13, 2022, www.thecrimson.com/article/2022/7/13/faculty-survey-political-leaning/

35 Phillip W. Magness and David Waugh, "The Hyperpoliticization of Higher Ed: Trends in Faculty Political Ideology, 1969–Present," *The Independent Review* (Winter 2022/23); Kevin Wallsten, "The Political Causes of Higher Education's Decline: Ideological Homogeneity and Radicalism on College Campuses Are Driving Away Potential Students," *City Journal*, December 4, 2025, www.city-journal.org/article/higher-education-decline-graduate-bachelors-degree.

36 Giroux.

37 Newfield, *The Great Mistake*.

38 Baldwin, *In the Shadow of the Ivory Tower*.

[39] Mazzucato, *The Entrepreneurial State*; Klein and Thompson, *Abundance.*

[40] Ibid.

[41] Ibid.

[42] Baldwin.

[43] Christopher J. Lucas, *Crisis in the Academy: The Plight of the American University* (New York: St. Martin's Press, 1998).

[44] Alyssa Hatfield, "Varsity Blues Scandal Explained: Lawyers provided a behind-the-scenes understanding of how the admissions scam worked," *Boston College Law Magazine*, December 5, 2023, lawmagazine.bc.edu/2023/12/varsity-blues-sandal-explained/; Caroline Blair, "How Was Brett Favre Involved in the Mississippi Welfare Scandal? Inside One of the Biggest Public Fraud Cases in History," *People*, May 21, 2025, 12, people.com/how-was-brett-favre-involved-in-welfare-scandal-11737440; Aaron Pellish, "Trump pardons real estate developer indicted under his own DOJ," Politico, December 3, 2025, www.politico.com/news/2025/12/03/trump-pardons-real-estate-developer-indicted-under-his-own-doj-00676253.

[45] Klein and Thompson.

[46] Anna Joukovskaia, "Bureaucracy: The Making of a Buzzword." *Journal of the History of Ideas* 84, no. 4 (2023): 685-710.

[47] Weber, *Economy and society.*

[48] Julia K. K. Lee, Brittany E. Charlton, Nicole M. Skinner, Samantha K. Busa, and Katelyn E. W. Jelinek, "A Systematic Review of Diversity, Equity, and Inclusion and Antiracism Training Studies: Findings and Future Directions," *PMC - NIH*, October 19, 2023, pmc.ncbi.nlm.nih.gov/articles/PMC10890819/; Sam Levin, "Sexual Harassment Training May Have Reverse Effect, Research Suggests," *The Guardian*, May 2, 2016, www.theguardian.com/us-news/2016/may/02/sexual-harassment-training-failing-women.

[49] Elizabeth Levy Paluck, Roni Porat, Chelsey S. Clark, and Donald P. Green, "Prejudice Reduction: Progress and Challenges," *Annual Review of Psychology* 72 (2021): 533–560, https://doi.org/10.1146/annurev-psych-071620-030619.

[50] Tammie Cumming, M. David Miller, and Isana Leshchinskaya, "DEI Institutionalization: Measuring Diversity, Equity, and Inclusion in Postsecondary Education," *The Clearing House: A Journal of Educational Strategies, Issues and Ideas* 96, no. 1 (February 2023): 35,

https://doi.org/10.1080/00091383.2023.2151802.

51 Lomotey and Smith, *The Racial Crisis in American Higher Education.*

52 Kimberly A. Griffin, "Redoubling Our Efforts: How Institutions Can Affect Faculty Diversity," in *Race and Ethnicity in Higher Education: A Status Report* (Washington, D.C.: American Council on Education, 2019), www.equityinhighered.org/wp-content/uploads/2019/02/REHE-Essay-Chapter-10-SA.pdf.

53 Lauryn Burnett and Herman Aguinis, "How to Prevent and Minimize DEI Backfire," *Business Horizons* 67, no. 2 (March–April 2024): 173–182; Legault, Jennifer N. Gutsell, and Michael Inzlicht, "Ironic Effects of Antiprejudice
Messages: How Motivational Interventions Can Reduce (but Also Increase) Prejudice," *Psychological Science* 22, no. 12 (2011), https://doi.org/10.1177/0956797611427918; Deborah L. Kidder et al., "Backlash Toward Diversity Initiatives: Examining the Impact of Diversity Program Justification, Personal and Group Outcomes," *International Journal of Conflict Management* 15, no. 1 (January 2004): 85, https://doi.org/10.1108/eb022908.

54 Kim Rueben and Sheila Murray, "Racial Disparities in Education Finance: Going Beyond Equal Revenues," Discussion Paper No. 29 (Washington, D.C.: Urban Institute, November 2008), 5, www.urban.org/sites/default/files/publication/32136/411785-Racial-Disparities-in-Education-Finance-Going-Beyond-Equal-Revenues.PDF; William "Sandy" Darity and Kirsten Mullen, "Black Reparations and the Racial Wealth Gap," Commentary, Brookings, June 15, 2020, accessed December 10, 2025, www.brookings.edu/articles/black-reparations-and-the-racial-wealth-gap/; Baker, *Educational Inequality and School Finance.*

55 Graeber, *The Utopia of Rules: On Technology, Stupidity, and the Secret Joys of Bureaucracy*, 184.

56 "Favorite signs your administrators have no idea what they are talking about? ," *Reddit,* www.reddit.com/r/Teachers/comments/11ecvsc/favorite_signs_your_admin istrators_have_no_idea/ ; "The dumbest conversation I ever had with an administrator," *Reddit,* www.reddit.com/r/Teachers/comments/17j1b8x/the_dumbest_conversation _i_ever_had_with_an/; "Shit Management Says," *X,* x.com/shitmgmtsays

57 Jon Marcus, "You've seen the meme. Here are some actual college administrator titles As academic bureaucracy grows deeper, here's who populates the layers," *Hechinger Report,* May 24, 2016 hechingerreport.org/youve-seen-meme-actual-college-administrator-titles/

[58] Generate Your Next Job Title Website pokes fun at administrative bloat by generating endless job titles and inflated salaries," *Inside Higher*

Education, May 17, 2016, www.insidehighered.com/news/2016/05/18/university-title-generator-website-pokes-fun-administrative-bloat

Chapter 2

[1] Nolan Higdon, "Being on the outside of the inside of the ivory tower: Nontenured part-time
faculty's attitudes toward their colleagues and management." *Journal of Education Human
Resources* 42, no. 2 (2024): 175-197.

[2] Ibid.

[3] American Association of University Professors (AAUP), "Appendix I: 1915 Declaration of Principles on Academic Freedom and Academic Tenure," accessed December 11, 2025, www.aaup.org/NR/rdonlyres/A6520A9D-0A9A-47B3-B550-C006B5B224E7/0/1915Declaration.pdf.

[4] American Association of University Professors (AAUP), "1940 Statement of Principles on Academic Freedom and Tenure with 1970 Interpretive Comments," accessed December 11, 2025, www.aaup.org/sites/default/files/1940%20Statement.pdf.

[5] Schleck, *Dirty Knowledge.*

[6] American Association of University Professors (AAUP), "FAQs on Academic Freedom," accessed December 11, 2025, www.aaup.org/issues-higher-education/academic-freedom/faqs-academic-freedom.

[7] Schleck

[8] M. J. Heale, "The Politics of Patriotism: Loyalty Oaths," in *McCarthy's Americans: Red Scare Politics in State and Nation, 1935–1965* (London: Macmillan Education UK, 1998).

[9] Michael Hiltzik, "Column: A reminder: Anti-communist hysteria almost destroyed the University of California," *Los Angeles Times*, May 12, 2017, www.latimes.com/business/hiltzik/la-fi-hiltzik-uc-communists-20170512-story.html.

[10] Hugh Grant, "Academic Contests? Merit Pay in Canadian Universities," *Relations
Industrielles/Industrial Relations* (1998): 647–66

[11] Ibid.; Givan and Lang, *Strike for the Common Good: Fighting for the Future of Public Education.*

[12] Schuster and Finkelstein, *The American Faculty.*

[13] Glenn Colby, "March 2023 Data Snapshot: Tenure and Contingency in US Higher Education," American Association of University Professors (AAUP), March 2023, 3,

www.aaup.org/sites/default/files/AAUP%20Data%20Snapshot.pdf.
[14] Ginsberg, *The Fall of the Faculty.*

[15] Childress, *The Adjunct Underclass: How America's Colleges Betrayed Their Faculty, Their Students, and Their Mission.*
[16] Kenneth H. Wapman, Samuel Zhang, Aaron Clauset, and Daniel B. Larremore, "Quantifying
Hierarchy and Dynamics in US Faculty Hiring and Retention," *Nature* 610 (2022): 120–27,
https://doi.org/10.1038/s41586-022-05222-x.
[17] Mir Ali Hosseini, "What Is Left in the Neoliberal University?," *New Politics*, October 15, 2021, newpol.org/what-is-left-in-the-neoliberal-university/.
[18] American Association of University Professors (AAUP), "The Annual Report on the Economic Status of the Profession, 2020–21," 2021, www.aaup.org/report/annual-report-economic-status-profession-2020-21; Jonathan Wilson, "The Typical U.S. College Professor Makes $3,556 per Course," *Blue Book*, August 7, 2021, bluebook.life/2021/08/07/the-typical-us-college-professor-makes-3556-per-course/.
[19] AAUP, "The Annual Report on the Economic Status of the Profession, 2020–21."
[20] Anonymous, "Treadmill to Oblivion: An Anonymous Instructor Describes 25 Years Working as an Adjunct," *Inside Higher Education*, May 11, 2015, www.insidehighered.com/advice/2015/05/11/essay-instructor-who-has-taught-adjunct-25-years.
[21] David Graeber, *Bullshit Jobs: The Rise of Pointless Work, and What We Can Do About It* (London: Penguin, 2019).
[22] AAUP, "1940 Statement."; Richard F. Teichgraeber III. "Tenure matters: A historian's perspective." *AAUP Journal of Academic Freedom* 14 (2014): 1-31.
[23] Teichgraeber III
[24] LooSee Beh, Susan Thomas, Qiu Ting Chie, Mathew Abraham, and Sony Jalarajan Raj. "A
Qualitative Review of Literature on Peer Review of Teaching in Higher Education." *Review of
Educational Research* 84 (2014): 112-159; Lily Min Zeng, "Peer review of teaching in higher
education: A systematic review of its impact on the professional development of university
teachers from the teaching expertise perspective." *Educational Research Review* 31 (2020):
100333.
[25] LooSee, et al.

26 Troy Heffernan, "Sexism, racism, prejudice, and bias: A literature review and synthesis of research surrounding student evaluations of

courses and teaching." *Assessment & Evaluation in Higher Education* 47, no. 1 (2022): 144-154.

27 Jamila Bookwala, Marc Falk, Jeanne Hamming, Stephanie Storms, and Bohsiu Wu. "Peer Review of Teaching: Should It Be the Gold Standard?" *The ACAD Leader*, April 2023. acad.org/resource/peer-review-of-teaching-should-it-be-the-gold-standard/.

28 Benjamin F. Jones, "The burden of knowledge and the "death of the renaissance man": Is

innovation getting harder?." *The Review of Economic Studies* 76, no. 1 (2009): 283-317.

29 Klein and Thompson.

30 Ibid.

31 Schleck

32 Mazzucato, *The Entrepreneurial State.*

33 Klein and Thompson

Chapter 3

1 Slaughter and Leslie, *Academic Capitalism.*

2 Bourdieu, *Distinction.*

3 Elizabeth Tandy Shermer, "Higher Ed's Past is Gilded, Not Golden," *Academe* (Fall 2022); Elizabeth Tandy Shermer, *Indentured Students: How Government-Guaranteed Loans Left Generations Drowning in College Debt* (Cambridge, MA: Harvard University Press, 2021)

4 Nikki Brahm, "How the GI Bill Has Evolved and Enabled Access to Higher Education," *Insight into Academia*, July 2, 2024, insightintoacademia.com/how-the-gi-bill-has-evolved-and-enabled-access-to-higher-education/.

5 Thelin, *A History of American Higher Education.*

6 Jerry Coughter and Conor Gowder, "Why Is the Cost of College Rising So Fast?," *SSTI (State Science & Technology Institute)*, September 19, 2024, ssti.org/blog/why-cost-college-rising-so-fast.

7 Ibid.

8 Ibid.

9 Lance Dinino '25, "Death By a Thousand Emails: How Administrative Bloat Is Killing American Higher Education," *The Bowdoin Review*, February 7, 2024, students.bowdoin.edu/bowdoin-review/features/death-by-a-thousand-emails-how-administrative-bloat-is-killing-american-higher-education/.

10 Peter L. Hinrichs, "Trends in Revenues at US Colleges and Universities, 1987–2013," *Economic Commentary* (EC 2017-05, Federal Reserve Bank of Cleveland, March 23, 2017),

www.clevelandfed.org/publications/economic-commentary/2017/ec-201705-trends-in-revenues-at-us-colleges-and-universities-1987-2013;

State Higher Education Executive Officers Association (SHEEO), "For the first time, state funding to public colleges exceeds per-student funding levels seen prior to the Great Recession," May 25, 2023, sheeo.org/shef_report_22/#:~:text=The%20student%20share%20decreased%20from,funded%20by%20students%20and%20families.
[11] Mary Ellen Flannery, "State Funding for Higher Education Still Lagging," *NEA Today*, October 25, 2022, www.nea.org/nea-today/all-news-articles/state-funding-higher-education-still-lagging
[12] Hacker and Dreifus, *Higher Education?*, 33.
[13] Kevin Shih, "Do international students crowd-out or cross-subsidize Americans in higher education?," *Journal of Public Economics* 156 (2017): 175.
[14] Archibald and Feldman, *Why Does College Cost So Much?*.
[15] Melanie Hanson, "College Tuition Inflation Rate," EducationData.org, last modified November 26, 2025, educationdata.org/college-tuition-inflation-rate.
[16] Paul Millerd, "Why Did People Stop Caring About Developing a Meaningful Philosophy of Life in the 1970s?," *Paul Millerd* (blog), December 15, 2020, pmillerd.com/1970-meaning-money/.
[17] Giroux, *Neoliberalism's War on Higher Education*.
[18] Aila Boyd, "Considering the Long-Term Impact of Rankings Changes," *Volt Education*, April 16, 2024, voltedu.com/features/marketing-branding/considering-the-long-term-impact-of-rankings-changes/.
[19] Zoya Alam, "We're Thinking About College Rankings All Wrong," *The Nation*, September 30, 2025, www.thenation.com/article/society/college-rankings-exclusivity/.
[20] Eleanor Eckerson Peters, "Newly Released Federal Student Outcomes Data Show More Detail, Provide Better Information, and Increase Transparency in Higher Education," *IHEP*, October 12, 2017, www.ihep.org/newly-released-federal-student-outcomes-data-show-more-detail-provide-better-information-and-increase-transparency-in-higher-education/.
[21] Rick Seltzer, "Wealthy colleges should just admit more students, one of their biggest critics says," *Higher Ed Dive*, February 3, 2023, www.highereddive.com/news/wealth-colleges-admit-more-students-critic-says/641375/.
[22] Hayes, *New Strategies in Higher Education Marketing*.
[23] Flannery, *How to Market a University*.
[24] Ibid.

[25] Berman, *Creating the Market University*.

[26] Joshua Hall, "Finding Our God-Terms," *LA Review of Books*, March 2, 2026, lareviewofbooks.org/article/mark-edmundson-literary-criticism-american-university-humanities-essay/

[27] Edmundson, *Why Teach?*, xvi.

[28] Edmundson, *The Heart Of The Humanities*, 384.

[29] John A. Davis and Mark Farrell, *The Market Oriented University: An Inquiry into the Nature of Higher Education Management and Leadership* (Cham: Palgrave Macmillan, 2018)

[30] Preston Mizell, "OU student's zero for Christian-based gender critique triggers congressional pushback over academic bias," *Fox News*, December 4, 2025, www.foxnews.com/us/ou-students-zero-christian-based-gender-critique-triggers-congressional-pushback-over-academic-bias.

[31] Keith B. Murray, "A Better Metaphor: The Student as Client," *Inside Higher Ed*, December 10, 2024, www.insidehighered.com/opinion/views/2024/12/10/student-client-not-customer-opinion.

[32] Catherine Rampell, "Many With New College Degree Find the Job Market Humbling," *New York Times*, May 18, 2011, www.nytimes.com/2011/05/19/business/economy/19grads.html.

[33] Cecilia Jones, "Harvard report warns of 'damaging' grade inflation, 60% of grades are A's," *The College Fix*, November 28, 2025, www.goacta.org/2025/11/harvard-university-damaging-grade-inflation/.

[34] *Real Time with Bill Maher*, season 23, episode 25, "September 5, 2025: Steven Pinker, Kaitlan Collins, Stephen Moore," September 5, 2025, HBO Max, www.hbomax.com/shows/real-time-with-bill-maher/s23/abc00905-6a23-46f6-a531-20214bb04bb06f37/e25-september-5-2025-steven-pinker-kaitlan-collins-stephen-moore/32ead0f8-d5a8-4a4f-9a79-649f0a330023.

[35] Donen, et al., *Grades Don't Matter*.

[36] *Real Time with Bill Maher*.

[37] Mark C. Perna, "New Data Reveals Just How Deep The College Crisis Goes," *Forbes*, January 28, 2025, www.forbes.com/sites/markcperna/2025/01/28/new-data-reveals-the-depth-of-college-crisis/.

[38] Ibid.

[39] Claire V. Miller, "It's Time for Harvard Students To Pick Up a Book," *The Harvard Crimson*, December 5, 2024, www.thecrimson.com/article/2024/12/5/miller-harvard-books-course-requirements/.

[40] Patricia R. Zimmermann, "The New Long COVID Is College Without Classes," *The Edge*, May 31, 2023, www.theedgemedia.org/new-long-covid-college-without-classes/.

[41] Ibid.

[42] Mark N. Lubell, "The Great Disengagement: Has COVID Transformed the Culture of Higher Education?" UC Davis Center for Environmental Policy and Behavior, May 18, 2022, environmentalpolicy.ucdavis.edu/news/great-disengagement-has-covid-tranformed-culture-higher-education; Sophie H. Cormack, Laurence A. Eagle, and Mark S. Davies, "A Large-Scale Test of the Relationship between Procrastination and Performance Using Learning Analytics," *Assessment & Evaluation in Higher Education* 45, no. 7 (2020): 1046–1059, doi.org/10.1080/02602938.2019.1705244; Melissa Bond, Katja Buntins, Svenja Bedenlier, Olaf Zawacki-Richter, and Michael Kerres, "Mapping Research in Student Engagement and Educational Technology in Higher Education: A Systematic Evidence Map," *International Journal of Educational Technology in Higher Education* 17, no. 2 (2020): 1–30, doi.org/10.1186/s41239-019-0176-8.

[43] George D. Kuh, John H. Schuh, Elizabeth J. Whitt, and Associates, *Involving Colleges: Successful Approaches to Fostering Student Learning and Personal Development Outside the Classroom* (San Francisco: Jossey-Bass, 1991).

[44] Zimmermann.

[45] Jean M. Twenge and W. Keith Campbell, *The Narcissism Epidemic: Living in the Age of Entitlement* (New York: Simon and Schuster, 2009).

[46] "Dunning–Kruger Effect," The Decision Lab, accessed December 26, 2024, thedecisionlab.com/biases/dunning-kruger-effect.

[47] Fatima Seeme, David Green, and Carlo Kopp, "Ignorance of the Crowd: Dysfunctional Thinking in Social Networks," *Frontiers in Communication* 10 (2025): 1547489, doi.org/10.3389/fcomm.2025.1547489; Douglas C. Youvan, "Confronting Willful Ignorance: Cognitive Biases, Social Media Echo Chambers, and the 'Conspiracy Theory' Phenomenon," (2024).

[48] Katy Steinmetz, "Milo Yiannopoulos Finally Spoke at Berkeley. But the Protesters Were Louder," *Time*, September 24, 2017, time.com/4955245/milo-yiannopoulos-berkeley-free-speech-week/; Saeed Ahmed and Jacque Wilson, "UC Berkeley Student Group Votes to Disinvite Bill Maher; College Overturns It," *CNN*, October 30, 2014, www.cnn.com/2014/10/30/living/bill-maher-commencement-speaker; "Richard Dawkins' Berkeley Event Cancelled for 'Islamophobia,'" *BBC News*, July 24, 2017, www.bbc.com/news/world-us-canada-40710165.

[49] Tim O'Donnell, "Students in the wealthiest districts are obtaining disability accommodations at much higher rates, report finds," *The Week*, July 30, 2019, theweek.com/speedreads/855921/students-wealthiest-districts-are-obtaining-disability-accommodations-much-higher-rates-report-finds.

[50] Alyssa Hatfield, "Varsity Blues Scandal Explained," *Boston College Law Magazine*, December 5, 2023, lawmagazine.bc.edu/2023/12/varsity-blues-sandal-explained/.

[51] Elsa Johnson "Nearly 40% of Stanford undergraduates claim they're disabled. I'm one of them," *The Times,* February 02 2026, https://www.thetimes.com/us/news-today/article/40-percent-stanford-undergraduates-claim-disabled-sw99r3k8c.

[52] Rose Horowitch, "Elite Colleges Have an Extra-Time-on-Tests Problem," *The Atlantic*, December 2, 2025, www.theatlantic.com/magazine/2026/01/elite-university-student-accommodation/684946/; Johnson.

[53] Horowitch.

[54] Johnson.

[55] Horowitch.

[56] Reddit user, comment on "I believe in accommodations but do they become more questionable every year?," r/Professors, September 15, 2025, www.reddit.com/r/Professors/comments/1n7u9v6/i_believe_in_accommodations_but_do_they_become/.

Chapter 4

[1] Hillary Rodham Clinton, *What Happened* (New York: Simon & Schuster, 2017).

[2] Frank, *Listen, Liberal*.

[3] Higdon and Huff, *United States of Distraction*; Mattei, *The Capital Order*; Frank; Nolan Higdon, "Why the Legacy Media Suddenly Sound like Bernie Sanders: Bernie Sanders Was Right," *Salon*, January 13, 2025, www.salon.com/2025/01/13/why-the-legacy-media-suddenly-sound-like-bernie-sanders/.

[4] U.S. President. Executive Order 13788. "Buy American and Hire American." *Federal Register* 82, no. 76 (April 21, 2017): 18837–18839. trumpwhitehouse.archives.gov/presidential-actions/presidential-executive-order-buy-american-hire-american/.

[5] Adam Harris, "Executive Order Falls Short of Some HBCU Leaders' Hopes," *Chronicle of Higher Education*, February 28, 2017, www.chronicle.com/article/executive-order-falls-short-of-some-hbcu-leaders-hopes/.

[6] Jessica Harris, "Betsy DeVos and Her Cone of Silence on For-Profit Colleges," *Brookings* (blog), February 14, 2017, www.brookings.edu/articles/betsy-devos-for-profit-colleges-education-america/.

[7] Stephenie Johnson, Neil Campbell, and Kami Spicklemire, "The Trump-DeVos Budget Would Dismantle Public Education, Hurting Vulnerable Kids, Working Families, and Teachers," *Center for American Progress*,

March 17, 2017, www.americanprogress.org/article/trump-devos-budget-dismantle-public-education-hurting-vulnerable-kids-working-families-teachers/.

[8] "I love the poorly educated"—Read Donald Trump's full Nevada victory speech," *QZ*, July 20, 2022, qz.com/623640/i-love-the-poorly-educated-read-donald-trumps-full-nevada-victory-speech

[9] William A. Galston and Clara Hendrickson, "The educational rift in the 2016 election," Brookings Institution, November 28, 2016, www.brookings.edu/articles/the-educational-rift-in-the-2016-election/.

[10] Liu, *Virtue Hoarders*.

[11] Andrew S. Ross, "Brooksley Born foresaw disaster but was silenced," *San Francisco Chronicle* (SFGate), December 5, 2010, www.sfgate.com/business/bottomline/article/Brooksley-Born-foresaw-disaster-but-was-silenced-2454453.php.

[12] Financial Industry Paid Millions to Obama Aide Share full article By Jeff Zeleny April 3, 2009 WASHIN www.nytimes.com/2009/04/04/us/politics/04disclose.html

[13] Samuel Benson, "Two decades later, Cornel West's critique of Larry Summers hits differently," POLITICO, November 20, 2025, 4:59 PM EST, www.politico.com/news/2025/11/20/larry-summers-cornel-west-harvard-scandal-00663517.

[14] Amanda Schaffer, "The Ghost of Larry Summers," *Slate*, July 4, 2008, slate.com/technology/2008/07/the-ghost-of-larry-summers.html.

[15] Edward Helmore, "Harvard to investigate Larry Summers's Epstein ties as he exits OpenAI board," *The Guardian*, November 19, 2025, 9:07 AM EST, www.theguardian.com/business/2025/nov/19/harvard-larry-summers-epstein-ties-openai.

[16] Nolan Higdon, "The Vaulted Gates: Intelligence, Impunity, and the Architecture of the Epstein Class," *Gaslight Gazette,* March 02, 2026, https://nolanhigdon.substack.com/p/the-vaulted-gates

[17] Spencer Brayton and Natasha Casey, "Not Tolerating Intolerance: Unpacking Critical Pedagogy in Classrooms and Conferences," in *Libraries Promoting Reflective Dialogue in a Time of Political Polarization*, edited by Andrea Baer, Ellysa Stern Cahoy, and Robert Schroeder (Chicago: ACRL Press, 2019), 171–186.

[18] Frances Maher and Mary Kay Thompson Tetreault. *Privilege and diversity in the academy.* (New York: Routledge, 2013).

[19] Newfield, *The Great Mistake*.

[20] Gabriella Gutiérrez y Muhs, Yolanda Flores Niemann, Carmen G. González, and Angela P. Harris, eds, *Presumed incompetent: The intersections of race and class for women in academia*, (University Press of Colorado, 2012); Isis H. Settles, Martinque K. Jones, NiCole T. Buchanan, and Sheila T. Brassel, "Epistemic exclusion of women faculty and faculty of color: Understanding scholar (ly) devaluation as a predictor of turnover intentions," *The Journal of Higher Education* 93, no. 1 (2022): 31-55.

[21] NAACP Legal Defense and Educational Fund, "Brown v. Board of Education: The Case that Transformed America," accessed December 15, 2025, www.naacpldf.org/brown-vs-board/.

[22] Philip F. Rubio, *A History of Affirmative Action, 1619–2000* (Jackson, MS: University Press of Mississippi, 2009).

[23] Pincus, *Reverse Discrimination*.

[24] Sonari Glinton, "The Real History Behind DEI And Workplace Equity In America," *Forbes*, June 26, 2025, 8:00 AM EDT, www.forbes.com/sites/sonariglinton/2025/06/26/the-real-history-behind-dei-and-workplace-equity-in-america/.

[25] Christian Parenti, "'Diversity' Is a Ruling-Class Ideology," *Compact Magazine*, January 19, 2023, compactmag.com/article/diversity-is-a-ruling-class-ideology.

[26] Nolan Higdon, "DEI in Name Only: Navigating the Gap between the Rhetoric and the Reality of Social Justice in Higher Education," *Protest* 5, no. 1 (2025): 135.

[27] Monica L. Wang, Alexis Gomes, Marielis Rosa, Phillipe Copeland, and Victor Jose Santana, "A systematic review of diversity, equity, and inclusion and antiracism training studies: Findings and future directions," *Translational Behavioral Medicine* 14, no. 3 (2024): 165, doi:10.1093/tbm/ibad061.

[28] DiAngelo, *White Fragility*.

[29] Ibid.

[30] Davarian L. Baldwin, *In the Shadow of the Ivory Tower: How Universities Are Plundering Our Cities* (New York: Bold Type Books, 2021).

[31] Martin Finkelstein, Valerie M. Conley, and Jack Schuster, "Taking the Measure of Faculty Diversity," TIAA Institute, April 2016, accessed December 15, 2025, www.tiaainstitute.org; Kathryn Palmer, "GAO Finds Faculty Diversity Lacking, Discrimination Complaint Processing Slow," *Inside Higher Ed*, April 10, 2024.

[32] Ayala Cohen and Yehuda Baruch, "Abuse and exploitation of doctoral students: A conceptual model for traversing a long and winding road to academia," *Journal of Business Ethics* 180, no. 2 (2022): 510,

doi.org/10.1007/s10551-021-04986-x.

[33] Kurt Andersen argues in *Fantasyland: How America Went Haywire: A 500-Year History* (New York: Random House, 2018).

[34] Elizabeth Martínez and Angela Y. Davis, "Coalition Building Among People of Color," *Inscriptions* 7 (1994): 45

[35] Rockhill, *Who Paid the Pipers of Western Marxism?*.

[36] Daniel Golden, *Spy Schools: How the CIA, FBI, and Foreign Intelligence Secretly Exploit America's Universities* (New York: Henry Holt and Co., 2017).

[37] Nolan Higdon, Decoding Epstein A Healthy Skeptic's Guide to the Epstein Saga, *Gaslight Gazette,* February 2026, nolanhigdon.substack.com/p/decoding-epstein

[38] Zine Magubane, "The Class Politics of Race," *Catalyst: A Journal of Theory & Strategy* 7, no. 2 (2023); Hughes, *The End of Race Politics*; Sowell, *Social Justice Fallacies*; Cornel West, "Cornel West on Corporate DEI Initiatives and Free Speech," YouTube video, 11:30, posted by Minds, July 13, 2022, accessed April 9, 2024, www.youtube.com/watch?v=ALuqMqzJYJI.

[39] Title IX of the Education Amendments of 1972, 20 U.S.C. § 1681 et seq.

[40] Gebser v. Lago Vista Independent School Dist., 524 U.S. 274 (1998).

[41] Davis v. Monroe County Bd. of Ed., 526 U.S. 629 (1999); Franklin v. Gwinnett County Public Schools, 503 U.S. 60 (1992).

[42] Joe Cohn, "New Title IX regulations carefully balance the rights of all students," *FIRE*, May 8, 2020, www.thefire.org/news/new-title-ix-regulations-carefully-balance-rights-all-students.

[43] U.S. Department of Education, Office for Civil Rights, *Dear Colleague Letter on Title IX* (September 22, 2017), archived on Clery Center, www.clerycenter.org/index.php?option=com_content&view=article&id=1 07:office-for-civil-rights-issues-dear-colleague-letter-on-title-ix&catid=24:blog&Itemid=159.

[44] Ronan Farrow, "From Aggressive Overtures to Sexual Assault: Harvey Weinstein's Accusers Tell Their Stories," *The New Yorker*, October 23, 2017; Jodi Kantor and Megan Twohey, "Harvey Weinstein Paid Off Sexual Harassment Accusers for Decades," *The New York Times*, October 5, 2017; Gretchen Carlson v. Roger Ailes, Complaint for Sexual Harassment (Superior Court of New Jersey, July 6, 2016); Megyn Kelly, *Settle for More* (New York: Harper, 2016); Lauren Sivan, "TV Journalist Lauren Sivan Opens Up About Harvey Weinstein, Roger Ailes," YouTube video, Megyn Kelly Today, May 9, 2018, accessed December 15, 2025, www.youtube.com/watch?v=zJSiuQSpub0.

[45] Tarana Burke, "Inception," *Me Too,* February 2026,

www.metoomvmt.org/get-to-know-us/history-inception/

[46] Lindsey Bever and Amy B Wang, "Brock Turner Freed after Serving Half of His Six-Month Jail Sentence for Sexual Assault," *The Washington Post*, September 2, 2016. www.washingtonpost.com/news/post-nation/wp/2016/09/01/after-brock-turners-soft-sentence-lawmakers-approve-stronger-punishments-for-sexual-assaults/

[47] *The Hunting Ground*, directed by Kirby Dick (2015; New York: Radius-TWC, 2015)

[48] *Roll Red Roll*, directed by Nancy Schwartzman (2018; New York: Kino Lorber, 2018)

[49] Zoe Ridolfi-Starr, "Transformation Requires Transparency: Critical Policy Reforms To Advance Campus Sexual Violence Response," *Yale Law Journal Forum* 125, May 2016, yalelawjournal.org/feature/transformation-requires-transparency; Gina Telega, "Why are Sexual Assaults on College Campuses Treated Differently?," Avalon Blog, June 15, 2018, avalonhealing.org/why-are-sexual-assaults-on-college-campuses-treated-differently/; Michelle J. Anderson, "Campus Sexual Assault Adjudication and Resistance to Reform," *Yale Law Journal Forum* 125, May 31, 2016, yalelawjournal.org/feature/campus-sexual-assault-adjudication-and-resistance-to-reform; Ilana Frier, "Campus sexual assault and due process," *Duke J. Const. L. & Pub. Pol'y Sidebar* 15 (2020): 117; "Sexual Assault on Campus: A Frustrating Search for Justice," Association of Health Care Journalists, accessed December 15, 2025, healthjournalism.org/contest-entry/sexual-assault-on-campus-a-frustrating-search-for-justice.

[50] "How Do Title IX Investigations Differ From Criminal Investigations?," *The Law Office of Brad C. Richardson, LLC*, Jul 29, 2025, www.bradrichardsonlawfirm.com/blog/how-do-title-ix-investigations-differ-from-criminal-investigations/; "Confidentiality Requirements," *Williams University*, February 25, 2026, titleix.williams.edu/confidentiality-privacy/confidentiality-requirements/

[51] Rose Miron and Lena Palacios, "Mandatory Reporting Policies Protect Universities, Not Survivors," *Gender Policy Report*, July 10, 2018 genderpolicyreport.umn.edu/mandatory-reporting-policies-protect-universities-not-survivors/

[52] *The Hunting Ground*, directed by Kirby Dick (2015; New York: Radius-TWC, 2015)

[53] Miron and Palacios.

[54] Ibid.

[55] *Fantastic Lies*, directed by Marina Zenovich, episode of *30 for 30*, ESPN, April 3, 2016,

[56] "The Fine Line Between A Bad Date And Sexual Assault: 2 Views On

Aziz Ansari," *All Things Considered*, NPR, January 16, 2018, www.npr.org/2018/01/16/578422491/the-fine-line-between-a-bad-date-and-sexual-assault-two-views-on-aziz-ansari.

[57] Meghan Downey, "The Trump Administration's New Title IX Rule," *The Regulatory Review*, May 20, 2020, www.theregreview.org/2020/05/20/downey-trump-administration-title-ix-rule/; Johanna Alonso, "Department of Education Reverts to Trump's Title IX Rule," *Inside Higher Ed*, February 3, 2025, www.insidehighered.com/news/government/politics-elections/2025/02/03/department-education-reverts-trumps-title-ix-rule.

[58] Alonso.

[59] Bartlett, et al, *Going the Distance*.

[60] Nolan Higdon and Allison Butler, "Mapping digital corporate media curriculum in the age of surveillance capitalism," *Review of Education, Pedagogy, and Cultural Studies* (Published online February 23, 2021): 390, doi.org/10.1080/10714413.2021.1877239.

[61] Higdon and Butler, *Surveillance Education*.

[62] Ibid.

[63] Ibid.

[64] Kristian Foden-Vencil, "College Rape Case Shows A Key Limit To Medical Privacy Law," *All Things Considered*, NPR, March 9, 2015, www.npr.org/sections/health-shots/2015/03/09/391876192/college-rape-case-shows-a-key-limit-to-medical-privacy-law.

[65] Nolan Higdon, "No Turning Back: We Cannot Reverse the Damage Done By Poor Pandemic Reporting, But The Fourth Estate Must Do Better," Substack, April 10, 2023, nolanhigdon.substack.com/p/no-turning-back.

[66] Ibid.; Julia M. Comeau, "A 'Noble Lie?' Dr. Anthony Fauci and Masking in the United States," Faculty Lead Archon Fung, *HKS Case Program*, August 13, 2025, case.hks.harvard.edu/a-noble-lie-dr-anthony-fauci-and-masking-in-the-united-states/.

[67] Ibid.

[68] "Black DC Residents REJECT Fauci To His Face On Vaccines," YouTube video, 11:39, posted by "Breaking Points," March 21, 2023, www.youtube.com/watch?v=27mr5PMYkKE; "Transcript: Dr. Anthony Fauci on 'Face the Nation,' May 16, 2021," interview by John Dickerson, *CBS News*, May 16, 2021, www.cbsnews.com/news/transcript-dr-anthony-fauci-face-the-nation-05-16-2021/; Higdon, "No Turning Back."

[69] Caleb Ecarma, "Joe Rogan and CNN Are Butting Heads Over 'Horse Dewormer' COVID Cure," *Vanity Fair*, October 22, 2021, www.vanityfair.com/news/2021/10/joe-rogan-cnn-horse-dewormer-covid.

[70] Higdon, "No Turning Back."

71 Lebron, *The Making of Black Lives Matter*; Taylor, *From #BlackLivesMatter to Black Liberation*; Johnson and Edgar, *The Summer of 2020*.

72 Luke Mogelson, "The Militias Against Masks," *The New Yorker*, August 17, 2020, www.newyorker.com/magazine/2020/08/24/the-militias-against-masks; Ken Coleman, "Report: BLM protests have not contributed to COVID-19 spread," *Michigan Advance*, July 9, 2020, michiganadvance.com/2020/07/09/report-blm-protests-have-not-contributed-to-covid-19-spread/.

73 Delgado and Stefancic, *Critical Race Theory*.

74 Gloria Ladson-Billings, "Toward a Theory of Culturally Relevant Pedagogy," *Harvard Educational Review* 65, no. 3 (1995)

75 Jim Downs, ed., *January 6 and the Politics of History* (Athens, GA: University of Georgia Press, 2024)

76 Matt Taibbi, "Marcuse-Anon: Cult of the Pseudo-Intellectual Reviewing 'Repressive Tolerance' and other works by Herbert Marcuse, the quack who became America's most influential thinker," *Racket News* (Substack), February 16, 2021, www.racket.news/p/marcuse-anon-cult-of-the-pseudo-intellectual-1d3.

77 Michael Levenson, "A Psychiatrist Invited to Yale Spoke of Fantasies of Shooting White People," *New York Times*, June 6, 2021, www.nytimes.com/2021/06/06/nyregion/yale-psychiatrist-aruna-khilanani.html.

78 Hughes.

79 Bari Weiss, "Meet the Renegades of the Intellectual Dark Web," *New York Times*, May 8, 2018, www.nytimes.com/2018/05/08/opinion/intellectual-dark-web.html.

80 PowerfulJRE, "Joe Rogan Experience #1081 - Bret Weinstein & Heather Heying," YouTube video, 2:52:48, February 21, 2018, http://www.youtube.com/watch?v=HYJFgyqs0sM; "Evergreen copes with fallout, months after 'Day of Absence' sparked national debate," *PBS NewsHour*, last modified January 7, 2018, 5:14 PM EST, www.pbs.org/newshour/show/evergreen-copes-with-fallout-months-after-day-of-absence-sparked-national-debate.

81 Susan D'Agostino, "Amid Backlash, Stanford Pulls 'Harmful Language' List," *Inside Higher Ed,* January 10, 2023, www.insidehighered.com/news/diversity/2023/01/10/amid-backlash-stanford-removes-harmful-language-list#

82 Ibid.

83 Ibid.

84 Ibid.

[85] PowerfulJRE, "Joe Rogan Experience #1191 - Peter Boghossian & James Lindsay," YouTube video, 2018, www.youtube.com/watch?v=0k571wE7xRk; Jennifer Schuessler, "Hoaxers Slip Breastaurants and Dog-Park Sex Into Journals," *New York Times*, October 4, 2018, www.nytimes.com/2018/10/04/arts/academic-journals-hoax.html.

[86] Jennifer Schuessler, "Hoaxers Slip Breastaurants and Dog-Park Sex Into Journals," *New York Times*, October 4, 2018, www.nytimes.com/2018/10/04/arts/academic-journals-hoax.html.

[87] Frederick Hess, "Democrats Have Lost Public Confidence on Education, but Republicans Haven't Gained It," *Education Next*, April 25, 2022, www.educationnext.org/democrats-have-lost-public-confidence-education-but-republicans-havent-gained-it/.

[88] Matt Taibbi, "Loudoun County, Virginia: A Culture War in Four Acts," *Racket News* (Substack), December 10, 2021, www.racket.news/p/loudoun-county-virginia-a-culture.

[89] James Kvaal, "Opinion: Biden Administration Opened 'New Chapter' on College Financing, Kvaal Says," *Higher Ed Dive*, January 17, 2025, www.highereddive.com/news/biden-administration-opened-new-chapter-on-college-financing-kvaal-says/737723/; Joe Rogan, "JRE MMA Show #122," *The Joe Rogan Experience*, audio podcast, September 8, 2022, Spotify, 1:45:30.

[90] Daniel Byman, Riley McCabe, Alexander Palmer, Catrina Doxsee, Mackenzie Holtz, and Delaney Duff, "Hamas's October 7 Attack: Visualizing the Data," Center for Strategic and International Studies, last modified December 19, 2023, www.csis.org/analysis/hamass-october-7-attack-visualizing-data.

[91] James Cook, "More than 70,000 killed in Gaza since Israel offensive began, Hamas-run health ministry says," BBC News, November 29, 2025, www.bbc.com/news/articles/c8e97kl240lo; MEE staff, "More than 100,000 Palestinians likely killed in Gaza, leading German institute says," *Middle East Eye*, November 25, 2025, www.middleeasteye.net/news/more-100000-palestinians-killed-gaza-leading-german-institute-says; Marium Ali, Alia Chughtai, and Muhammet Okur, "Two years of Israel's genocide in Gaza: By the numbers," Al Jazeera, October 7, 2025, www.aljazeera.com/news/2025/10/7/two-years-of-israels-genocide-in-gaza-by-the-numbers.

[92] Jonathan Masters and Will Merrow, "U.S. Aid to Israel in Four Charts," Council on Foreign Relations, last updated October 7, 2025, www.cfr.org/article/us-aid-israel-four-charts; James J. Zogby, "Biden's Legacy: Complicity in Israel's Gaza War," Arab American Institute,

www.aaiusa.org/library/bidens-legacy-complicity-in-israels-gaza-war.

[93] Clare Duffy and Ramishah Maruf, "Columbia student protesters are demanding divestment. Here's what the university has divested from in the past," CNN, updated April 29, 2024, www.cnn.com/2024/04/27/business/columbia-history-divestment-student-protests.

[94] Abdallah Fayyad, "The lessons from colleges that didn't call the police," *Vox*, May 3, 2024, 2:00 PM PDT, www.vox.com/24147461/columbia-gaza-encampment-campus-protests-police-crackdown-pro-palestinian-students.

[95] Sarah Huddleston, "In leaked messages, members of 'Columbia Alumni for Israel' group chat work to identify, punish pro-Palestinian protesters," *Columbia Spectator*, March 5, 2025, www.columbiaspectator.com/news/2025/03/05/in-leaked-messages-members-of-columbia-alumni-for-israel-group-chat-work-to-identify-punish-pro-palestinian-protesters/; Matt Luo, "Columbia Advisory Committee on Socially Responsible Investing rejects Israel divestment proposals," *Columbia Spectator*, November 16, 2025, www.columbiaspectator.com/news/2025/11/16/columbia-advisory-committee-on-socially-responsible-investing-rejects-israel-divestment-proposals/.

[96] Andersen, *The Complicit Lens*.

[97] Erin Alberty, "Sen. Romney links TikTok ban to pro-Palestinian content," *Axios*, May 6, 2024, www.axios.com/local/salt-lake-city/2024/05/06/senator-romney-antony-blinken-tiktok-ban-israel-palestinian-content.

[98] Matt Schiavenza, "Had It with Higher Ed: Bill Maher Says U.S. Is Opening Its Eyes, College Now Makes Us Stupid," *Medium*, May 1, 2024, medium.com/leadership-culture/had-it-with-higher-ed-bill-maher-says-u-s-is-opening-its-eyes-college-now-makes-us-stupid-eae467b48705.

[99] Jay Ulfelder, "Crowd Counting Consortium: An Empirical Overview of Recent Pro-Palestine Protests at U.S. Schools," Harvard Kennedy School Ash Center for Democratic Governance and Innovation, May 30, 2024, ash.harvard.edu/articles/crowd-counting-blog-an-empirical-overview-of-recent-pro-palestine-protests-at-u-s-schools/.

[100] Carter Castillo, Vivian Dueker, Raymond Tran, and Guardian Staff, "UCSD's Gaza Solidarity Encampment: Students face interim suspensions, counter-protests continue, and campus groups respond," *UCSD Guardian*, May 5, 2024, ucsdguardian.org/2024/05/05/ucsds-gaza-solidarity-encampment-students-face-interim-suspensions-counter-protests-continue-and-campus-groups-respond/; Susan Snyder and Beatrice Forman, "Penn weighs risk of removing encampment, saying it 'is causing fear for

many'," *Philadelphia Inquirer*, updated May 6, 2024, 6:42 p.m. ET, www.inquirer.com/education/upenn-statement-campus-protests-encampments-20240506.html.

[101] American Library Association, "Hate Speech and Hate Crime," last modified December 2017, www.ala.org/advocacy/intfreedom/hate.

[102] American Civil Liberties Union, "Speech on Campus," December 18, 2023, www.aclu.org/documents/speech-campus.

[103] Matthew Ormseth et al., "UCLA struggles to recover after 200 arrested, pro-Palestinian camp torn down," *Los Angeles Times*, published May 1, 2024, updated May 3, 2024, 10:18 AM PT, www.latimes.com/california/story/2024-05-01/la-me-ucla-camp-police.

[104] Juan Perez Jr., "Campus free speech is getting murky for Republican governors," *Politico*, April 27, 2024, 7:00 AM EDT, www.politico.com/news/2024/04/27/republican-states-colleges-free-speech-israel-gaza-complicated-00154702.

[105] Teresa Watanabe, "USC cancels May in-person graduation. What about UCLA and other colleges?," *Los Angeles Times*, March 20, 2020, 6:53 PM PT, www.latimes.com/california/story/2020-03-20/ucla-reconsiders-coronavirus-graduation-cancellation-what-are-other-colleges-doing.

[106] CAIR San Francisco Bay Area, "CAIR Designates UC Berkeley a 'Hostile Campus' for Systematic Suppression of Anti-Genocide Speech," news release, August 26, 2025, ca.cair.com/press-release/cair-designates-uc-berkeley-a-hostile-campus-for-systematic-suppression-of-anti-genocide-speech/.

[107] Noah Hurowitz, "UN Experts Blast U.S. Universities for Human Rights Violations Against Gaza Protesters," *The Intercept*, December 16, 2025, theintercept.com/2025/12/16/un-human-rights-universities-columbia-gaza-protests/.

[108] Andrew Lapin/JTA, "Opposing Trump's campus policies as a Jewish university president," *Jerusalem Post*, October 17, 2025, 00:14, www.jpost.com/diaspora/article-870741; Steven Mintz, "Protest, Power and the Future of the University," *Inside Higher Ed*, March 31, 2025, www.insidehighered.com/opinion/columns/higher-ed-gamma/2025/03/31/why-gaza-became-defining-campus-flashpoint.

[109] Natasha Lennard, "University Professors Are Losing Their Jobs Over "New McCarthyism" on Gaza," *The Intercept*, May 16, 2024, 5:00 a.m., theintercept.com/2024/05/16/university-college-professors-israel-palestine-firing/; Alice Speri, "The chilling effect of Title VI investigations: the professors accused of antisemitism," *Guardian*, September 11, 2025, www.theguardian.com/us-news/2025/sep/11/campus-investigations-professors-gaza-antisemitism; Ryan Quinn, "DePaul Adjunct Ousted for

Optional Gaza Assignment," *Inside Higher Ed*, June 3, 2024, www.insidehighered.com/news/faculty-issues/academic-freedom/2024/06/03/depaul-adjunct-ousted-optional-gaza-assignment; *The Intercept*, "CUNY professors say they were fired for Palestine support," *University World News*, July 20, 2025, www.universityworldnews.com/post.php?story=20250719104319562; and Rutgers AAUP-AFT, "Immediately Reinstate CUNY Adjunct Faculty Terminated for Standing with Palestinians," September 2, 2025, rutgersaaup.org/immediately-reinstate-cuny-adjunct-faculty-terminated-for-standing-with-palestinians/.

[110] Lauren Camera, "Education Department Says 2 Universities Failed to Protect Jewish, Muslim Students," *U.S. News & World Report*, June 17, 2024, www.usnews.com/news/education-news/articles/2024-06-17/education-department-says-2-schools-failed-to-protect-jewish-muslim-students; Anti-Defamation League, "Audit of Antisemitic Incidents 2024," 2024, www.adl.org/resources/report/audit-antisemitic-incidents-2024; Graham Wright, "Antisemitism on Campus Is a Real Problem — But Headlines and Government-Proposed Solutions Don't Match the Experience of Most Jewish Students," *The Conversation*, September 19, 2025, theconversation.com/antisemitism-on-campus-is-a-real-problem-but-headlines-and-government-proposed-solutions-dont-match-the-experience-of-most-jewish-students-265041.

[111] Council on American-Islamic Relations, California (CAIR-CA), "CPHB Release 2024 Campus Climate Report Highlighting Rise in Islamophobia on College Campuses," press release, November 19, 2024, www.cair.com/press_releases/cair-ca-cphb-release-2024-campus-climate-report-highlighting-rise-in-islamophobia-on-college-campuses/; Camera; Zachary Schermele, "As Trump Clamps Down, Harvard Finds Evidence of Antisemitism, Islamophobia on Campus," *USA Today*, updated April 29, 2025, www.usatoday.com/story/news/education/2025/04/29/harvard-antisemitism-islamophobia-review-trump/83351766007/.

[112] CAIR San Francisco Bay Area, "CAIR Designates UC Berkeley a 'Hostile Campus'."

[113] UN Human Rights Office, "Israel Has Committed Genocide in the Gaza Strip, UN Commission Finds," September 16, 2025, www.ohchr.org/en/press-releases/2025/09/israel-has-committed-genocide-gaza-strip-un-commission-finds

[114] Pat McGuire, "3 Presidents Walk Into a Trap and We All Suffer," *Trinity Washington University*, December 10, 2023, discover.trinitydc.edu/president/2023/12/10/3-presidents-walk-into-a-trap-and-we-all-suffer/.

[115] Associated Press, "Kamala Harris' husband says elite college

presidents' 'lack of moral clarity is simply unacceptable'," *Business Insider*, December 8, 2023, 7:33 AM PT, www.businessinsider.com/emhoff-college-presidents-antisemitism-testimony-showed-lack-of-moral-clarity-2023-12; and Meg Woolhouse, "Harvard, MIT, Penn presidents face backlash after congressional hearing," WGBH, December 8, 2023, updated April 3, 2024, www.wgbh.org/news/education-news/2023-12-08/harvard-mit-penn-presidents-face-backlash-after-congressional-hearing

Chapter 5

[1] Michael T. Nietzel, "Gallup: Public Perception of a College Education Hits a 15-Year Low," *Forbes*, September 13, 2025, www.forbes.com/sites/michaeltnietzel/2025/09/13/gallup-public-perception-of-a-college-education-hits-a-15-year-low/.

[2] Ben Kamisar, "Poll: In a dramatic shift, Americans no longer see four-year college degrees as worth the cost," *NBC,* Nov. 28, 2025, www.nbcnews.com/politics/politics-news/poll-dramatic-shift-americans-no-longer-see-four-year-college-degrees-rcna243672

[3] Pew Research Center, "Partisanship by Race, Ethnicity and Education," April 9, 2024, in *Changing Partisan Coalitions in a Politically Divided Nation*, www.pewresearch.org/politics/2024/04/09/partisanship-by-race-ethnicity-and-education/.

[4] Anna Commander, "Democrat Net Favorability Plunges to Near Three-Decade Low, Poll Shows," *Newsweek*, August 7, 2025, www.newsweek.com/democrat-net-favorability-plunges-near-three-decade-low-poll-shows-2110513.

[5] Collin Binkley, "Trump Promised to End 'Wokeness' in Education. He Has Promised to Use Federal Funds as Leverage," *PBS NewsHour*, November 15, 2024, www.pbs.org/newshour/politics/trump-promised-to-end-wokeness-in-education-he-has-promised-to-use-federal-funds-as-leverage.

[6] Ishena Robinson, "How Woke Went From 'Black' to 'Bad,'" *Legal Defense Fund*, accessed December 17, 2025, www.naacpldf.org/woke-black-bad/; Ilya Shapiro, "How the Rise of Woke 'Educrats' Is Destroying Higher Education," *New York Post*, January 11, 2025, manhattan.institute/article/how-the-rise-of-woke-educrats-is-destroying-higher-education; "The Proper Reaction to the 'Woke' Conundrum in Higher Education," Letters to the Editor, *Washington Post*, October 29, 2025, www.washingtonpost.com/opinions/2025/10/29/woke-data-center-ai-energy-costs/.

[7] White House, "Fact Sheet: President Donald J. Trump Empowers Parents, States, and Communities to Improve Education Outcomes," March 20, 2025, www.whitehouse.gov/fact-sheets/2025/03/fact-sheet-president-donald-j-trump-empowers-parents-states-and-communities-to-improve-

184

education-outcomes/.

8 Samuel G. Freedman, "The Inconvenient Scholarship of Kevin Roberts," *Los Angeles Review of Books*, September 29, 2024, lareviewofbooks.org/article/the-inconvenient-scholarship-of-kevin-roberts/.

9 Horowitz, *The Professors*; D'Souza, *Illiberal Education*.

10 Nolan Higdon, "Charlie Kirk's Death: Media and Politics Spotlight America's Deepest Divides," *Nolan Higdon's Substack*, September 12, 2025, nolanhigdon.substack.com/p/charlie-kirks-death.

11 Yasin Gungor, "Trump Vows to End 'Woke' Ideology in Universities, Threatens Enforcement," *Anadolu Agency*, October 13, 2025, www.aa.com.tr/en/americas/trump-vows-to-end-woke-ideology-in-universities-threatens-enforcement/3715326.

12 Brooke Schultz, "President Trump's Early Actions Undo Biden Efforts to Protect LGBTQ+ Students," *Education Week*, January 20, 2025, www.edweek.org/policy-politics/president-trumps-early-actions-undo-biden-efforts-to-protect-lgbtq-students/2025/01; White House, "Ending Radical and Wasteful Government DEI Programs and Preferencing," January 20, 2025, www.whitehouse.gov/presidential-actions/2025/01/ending-radical-and-wasteful-government-dei-programs-and-preferencing/; White House, "Ending Illegal Discrimination and Restoring Merit-Based Opportunity," January 21, 2025, www.whitehouse.gov/presidential-actions/2025/01/ending-illegal-discrimination-and-restoring-merit-based-opportunity/; Laurie Witek, "Trump Administration Announces New Enforcement Efforts Targeted at DEI," *Dinsmore & Shohl LLP*, May 22, 2025, www.dinsmore.com/publications/trump-administration-announces-new-enforcement-efforts-targeted-at-dei/.

13 Reuters, "Font of 'Wasteful' Diversity: Trump's State Department Orders Return to Times New Roman," *The Guardian*, December 10, 2025, www.theguardian.com/us-news/2025/dec/10/trump-times-new-roman-font-return-state-department.

14 Johanna Alonso, "DOJ Report Declares MSIs Unconstitutional," *Inside Higher Ed*, December 22, 2025, www.insidehighered.com/news/institutions/minority-serving-institutions/2025/12/22/doj-report-declares-msis.

15 Ken Dilanian Alexandra Marquez, Claretta Bellamy, and Dan De Luce, "Federal Agencies Bar Black History Month and Other 'Special Observances,'" *NBC News*, January 31, 2025, last modified February 3, 2025, www.nbcnews.com/politics/donald-trump/defense-agency-bans-black-history-month-rcna190189.

16 Cheyanne M. Daniels, "Trump Moves to Repeal Disparate Impact

Liability, a Key Civil Rights Tenet," *The Hill*, April 24, 2025, thehill.com/homenews/administration/5265021-donald-trump-executive-orders-disparate-impact-civil-rights/; Sam Hananel, "The Truth About Disparate Impact and Equity," Center for American Progress, August 13, 2025, www.americanprogress.org/article/the-truth-about-disparate-impact-and-equity/.

[17] Donald J. Trump, "Executive Order 14168: Defending Women from Gender Ideology Extremism and Restoring Biological Truth to the Federal Government," January 20, 2025, *Federal Register* 90, no. 20 (January 30, 2025): 8615, www.whitehouse.gov/presidential-actions/2025/01/defending-women-from-gender-ideology-extremism-and-restoring-biological-truth-to-the-federal-government/.
[18] Sunlen Serfaty, "'It's a Black Hole': Civil Rights Office at Department of Education Veers from Original Mission," *CNN*, December 12, 2025, www.cnn.com/2025/12/12/politics/education-department-civil-rights-office-mission.
[19] Katherine Knott, "Sexual Violence Prevention Groups Criticize OCR's Handling of Title IX Cases," *Inside High Ed,* February 24, 2026, https://www.insidehighered.com/news/quick-takes/2026/02/24/coalition-criticizes-ocrs-handling-title-ix-cases
[20] Merlyn Thomas and Mike Wendling, "Trump Repeats Baseless Claim About Haitian Immigrants Eating Pets," *BBC News*, September 15, 2024, www.bbc.com/news/articles/c77l28myezko; Domenico Montanaro, "Without Apology, Trump Now Says: 'Obama Was Born In' The U.S.," *NPR*, September 16, 2016, www.npr.org/2016/09/16/494231757/without-apology-trump-now-says-obama-was-born-in-the-u-s; Amanda Holpuch, "Fact-checking Donald Trump's Recent Claims, from Mexico to San Francisco," *The Guardian*, July 7, 2015, www.theguardian.com/us-news/reality-check/2015/jul/07/fact-checking-donald-trump.
[21] Micaela McConnell and Steven Hubbard, "Learning in the Shadows: How Immigration Enforcement Harms Students and Schools," *American Immigration Council* (blog), August 26, 2025, www.americanimmigrationcouncil.org/blog/immigration-enforcement-harms-students-schools/.
[22] Sara Weissman, "If ICE Won't Show a Warrant, What Can Campuses Do?," *Inside Higher Education,* February 27, 2026, www.insidehighered.com/news/government/politics-elections/2026/02/27/if-ice-wont-show-warrant-what-can-campuses-do
[23] Memo Torres, "Fifteen U.S. Citizens Detained In Over 96 'Kavanaugh Stops,' As Feds Disregard Legal Documentation," *L.A. Taco*, December 8, 2025, lataco.com/kavanaugh-stops-legal-documentation; Dahlia Lithwick

and Mark Joseph Stern, "A Judge Just Drew the Line on the Supreme Court's Terrible 'Kavanaugh Stops' Decision," *Slate*, December 7, 2025, slate.com/news-and-politics/2025/12/judge-roasts-supreme-court-kavanaugh-stops.html.

[24] Natalie Schwartz, "Court Declines to Block DOGE from Accessing Education Department Data," *Higher Ed Dive*, February 18, 2025, www.highereddive.com/news/court-declines-block-doge-access-student-data/740274/; Mark Keierleber, "Trump's Massive Deportation Database Puts Students at Risk, Advocates Warn," *The 74*, May 8, 2025, www.the74million.org/article/trumps-massive-deportation-database-puts-students-at-risk-advocates-warn/; Audrey Watters, "Building Anti-Surveillance Ed-Tech," *Hack Education*, July 20, 2020, hackeducation.com/2020/07/20/surveillance; Nolan Higdon and Allison Butler, *Surveillance Education: Navigating the Conspicuous Absence of Privacy in Schools*, 1st ed. (Routledge, 2025).

[25] White House, "Fact Sheet: President Donald J. Trump Reforms Accreditation to Strengthen Higher Education," April 23, 2025, www.whitehouse.gov/fact-sheets/2025/04/fact-sheet-president-donald-j-trump-reforms-accreditation-to-strengthen-higher-education/.

[26] Ibid.

[27] Katherine Knott, "Trump's 'Secret Weapon'? College Accreditation," *Inside Higher Ed*, May 4, 2023, www.insidehighered.com/news/government/politics-elections/2023/05/04/trump-pledges-fire-radical-left-college-accreditors.

[28] U.S. Department of Education, "U.S. Department of Education to Update Accreditation Handbook to Support High-Quality, High-Value Education," press release, December 10, 2025, www.ed.gov/about/news/press-release/us-department-of-education-update-accreditation-handbook-support-high-quality-high-value-education.

[29] Alex Wolf, Patrick F. Linehan, Karima Maloney, Dwight J. Draughon, Drew Padley, and Tyler Evans, "White House Looks to Seize Control of Higher Education Policy Through 'Compact for Academic Excellence in Higher Education,'" *Client Alerts*, Steptoe LLP, October 23, 2025, www.steptoe.com/en/news-publications/white-house-looks-to-seize-control-of-higher-education-policy-through-compact-for-academic-excellence-in-higher-education.html.

[30] Regina Sienra, "U.S. Government To No Longer Regard Architecture, Education, and Nursing as Professional Degrees," *My Modern Met*, December 1, 2025, mymodernmet.com/professional-degrees-loans-archictecture-education/; Jessica Blake, "What to Know About Trump's Definition of Professional Degrees," *Inside Higher Ed*, November 26, 2025,

www.insidehighered.com/news/government/student-aid-policy/2025/11/26/what-know-about-definition-professional-degree.
[31] Vimal Patel, "Professors Are Being Watched: 'We've Never Seen This Much Surveillance'," *New York Times*, February 4, 2026, www.nytimes.com/2026/02/04/us/professors-classroom-surveillance-politics.html.
[32] Ibid.

[33] Emma Whitford, "Tenure Under Threat A spate of firings in the fall revealed just how corroded tenure protections have become. How did we get here?, *Inside Higher Ed,* January 26, 2026, https://www.insidehighered.com/news/faculty-issues/tenure/2026/01/26/tenure-under-threat; Michael T. Nietzel, "4 More States Ramp Up Their Attacks On Faculty Tenure," *Forbes,* February 18, 2026, https://www.forbes.com/sites/michaeltnietzel/2026/02/18/four-more-states-ramp-up-their-attacks-on-faculty-tenure/
[34] Christopher F. Rufo, "How DEI Corrupts America's Universities," *City Journal*, June 23, 2024, www.city-journal.org/article/how-dei-corrupts-americas-universities.
[35] Jessica Washington, "New Legal Documents Show Marco Rubio Targeted Students for Op-Eds and Protesting," *Intercept,* January 23 2026, theintercept.com/2026/01/23/mahmoud-khalil-palestine-protest-rubio/; Brett Wilkins, "'Confirming Everything We Knew Already': Docs Show Trump Admin Targeted Gaza Activists for Their Opinions," *Common Dreams,* Jan 23, 2026 www.commondreams.org/news/trump-free-speech-palestine
[36] TRT World, "Mohsen Mahdawi, Pro-Palestine Student Freed from ICE Custody, Graduates from Columbia," May 19, 2025, www.trtworld.com/article/ddd52229ca90; Mirna Alsharif, "Cornell University Student Activist Whose Visa Was Revoked Announces Departure from the U.S.," *NBC News*, April 1, 2025, last modified April 4, 2025, www.nbcnews.com/news/us-news/cornell-momodou-taal-visa-left-us-rcna199088.
[37] Associated Press, "Tufts Student Can Resume Research After Trump Officials Revoked Her Visa, Judge Rules," *The Guardian*, December 9, 2025, www.theguardian.com/us-news/2025/dec/09/rumeysa-ozturk-tufts-student-resume-teaching-visa.
[38] Sophie Bates and Philip Marcelo, "'Justice Prevailed but It's Very Long Overdue,' Mahmoud Khalil Says After His Ordered Release," *PBS NewsHour*, June 21, 2025, www.pbs.org/newshour/politics/watch-justice-prevailed-but-its-very-long-overdue-mahmoud-khalil-says-after-his-ordered-release.

[39] Jaclyn Diaz, "What We Know About the Case of Detained Georgetown Professor Badar Khan Suri," *NPR*, March 21, 2025, www.npr.org/2025/03/21/nx-s1-5336173/immigration-georgetown-university-professor.

[40] White House, "Countering Domestic Terrorism and Organized Political Violence," Presidential Memoranda, September 25, 2025, www.whitehouse.gov/presidential-actions/2025/09/countering-domestic-terrorism-and-organized-political-violence/.

[41] Ellie Davis, Gavin Escott, and Claire Murphy, "Employees and Students at These Colleges Have Been Punished for Comments on Charlie Kirk's Death," *Chronicle of Higher Education*, September 22, 2025, www.chronicle.com/article/employees-and-students-at-these-colleges-have-been-punished-for-comments-on-charlie-kirks-death.

[42] Emma Whitford, "N.C. Community College Fires Professor for Kirk Comments," *Inside Higher Ed,* February 24, 2026, https://www.insidehighered.com/news/quick-takes/2026/02/24/nc-community-college-fires-professor-kirk-comments

[43] Ayden Runnels, "Student Who Mocked Charlie Kirk's Death 'No Longer' at Texas State University as Clampdowns Continue," *Texas Tribune*, September 16, 2025, www.texastribune.org/2025/09/16/texas-state-university-student-charlie-kirk-comments/; KCBD Digital and Akim Powell, "College Student Expelled After Alleged Video of Her Celebrating Charlie Kirk's Death Went Viral," *KPTV*, September 15, 2025, www.kptv.com/2025/09/15/college-student-expelled-after-alleged-video-her-celebrating-charlie-kirks-death-went-viral/.

[44] Michael C. Bender and Stephanie Saul, "Trump Administration Sends Harvard a List of Demands to Protect Federal Funds," *New York Times*, April 3, 2025, www.nytimes.com/2025/04/03/us/politics/trump-harvard-funding-demands.html; Dwight J. Draughon, Patrick F. Linehan, Alex Wolf, and Evelyn Hudson, "A New Federal Playbook for Higher Education Oversight," *Steptoe*, August 7, 2025, www.steptoe.com/en/news-publications/a-new-federal-playbook-for-higher-education-oversight.html; Nate Raymond, "US Judge Blocks Defense Department from Slashing Federal Research Funding," *USA Today*, June 17, 2025, www.usatoday.com/story/news/politics/2025/06/17/pentagon-federal-research-funding-court-ruling/84249274007/; Department of Energy, "Department of Energy Overhauls Policy for College and University Research, Saving $405 Million Annually for American Taxpayers," April 11, 2025, www.energy.gov/articles/department-energy-overhauls-policy-college-and-university-research-saving-405-million; Kara Arundel, "House Committee Approves 25% Cut to Title I," *K12 Dive*, July 11, 2024,

www.k12dive.com/news/house-committee-25-cut-to-title-i-schools-FY25/721077/; Lasherica Thornton, "High-Needs Students: AmeriCorps Cuts Slash Support Services, Programs for Vulnerable Communities," *EdSource*, May 2, 2025, edsource.org/2025/americorps-cuts-slash-support-services-programs-for-vulnerable-communities/731928; Jessica Blake, "What Happened to the Smaller Agencies Trump Tried to Shutter?" *Inside Higher Ed*, July 16, 2025, www.insidehighered.com/news/government/science-research-policy/2025/07/16/neh-americorps-and-others-face-financial-freezes; Ryan

Quinn and Katherine Knott, "$900 Million in Institute of Education Sciences Contracts Axed," *Inside Higher Ed*, February 12, 2025, www.insidehighered.com/news/faculty-issues/research/2025/02/12/900m-institute-education-sciences-contracts-axed.

[45] Justine McDaniel and Susan Svrluga, "Trump vs. Harvard: A Timeline of How the Fight Escalated," *Washington Post*, December 2, 2025, www.washingtonpost.com/education/interactive/2025/timeline-trump-harvard/; Patrick F. Linehan, Alex Wolf, Dwight J. Draughon, Jr., Tyler Evans, and Emma Howard, "Universities Face Full Funding Freezes Amid Trump Administration Demands," *Steptoe*, April 25, 2025, www.steptoe.com/en/news-publications/universities-face-full-funding-freezes-amid-trump-administration-demands.html.

[46] Associated Press, "Penn to Ban Trans Women from Women's Sports, Ends Case Focused on Lia Thomas," *ESPN*, July 1, 2025, www.espn.com/college-sports/story/_/id/45634254/penn-ban-trans-athletes-ending-lia-thomas-civil-rights-case; Jake Offenhartz, "Columbia University Agrees to Policy Changes after Trump Administration Funding Threats," *PBS NewsHour*, March 21, 2025, www.pbs.org/newshour/education/columbia-university-agrees-to-policy-changes-after-trump-administration-funding-threats; Brown University, "Federal Agreement FAQs: Brown's Sex and Gender Policies and Gender-Affirming Care," Office of Equity Compliance and Reporting, accessed December 17, 2025, campus-life.brown.edu/oecr/faq-sex-and-gender; Sam Levin, "UC Berkeley Shares 160 Names with Trump Administration in 'McCarthy Era' Move," *The Guardian*, September 12, 2025, www.theguardian.com/us-news/2025/sep/12/uc-berkeley-trump-administration-antisemitism.

[47] Josh Moody, "Policy Changes and Financial Issues Drove November Cuts," *Inside Higher Ed*, December 3, 2025, www.insidehighered.com/news/business/financial-health/2025/12/03/policy-and-financial-issues-drove-november-cuts.

[48] Jordan Friedman, "The Rise and Rapid Fall of the First US Department

of Education," *History,* September 05, 2025,
www.history.com/articles/department-education-andrew-johnson-
reconstruction

[49] Ryan Quinn, "Trump's Effort to Break Up Education Dept. Part of Long History," *Inside Higher Ed*, November 24, 2025, www.insidehighered.com/news/government/2025/11/24/trump-isnt-first-president-try-break-ed.

[50] U.S. Department of Education, "U.S. Department of Education Announces Six New Agency Partnerships to Break Up Federal Bureaucracy," press release, November 18, 2025, www.ed.gov/about/news/press-release/us-department-of-education-announces-six-new-agency-partnerships-break-federal-bureaucracy.

[51] Times Now Digital, "What Department of Education Does and Why Donald Trump Wants to Shut It | EXPLAINED," *MSN*, March 2025, www.msn.com/en-in/news/world/what-department-of-education-does-and-why-donald-trump-wants-to-shut-it-explained/ar-AA1AolRF; Maria Danilova, "Trump's New Federal Cleanout Target: The Education Department," *Barron's*, February 9, 2025, www.barrons.com/news/trump-s-new-federal-cleanout-target-the-education-department-74b2ed94.

[52] Cheyenne Haslett, "What Will Dismantling the Education Department Mean for Your Student Loans?" *ABC News*, February 12, 2025, abcnews.go.com/Politics/dismantling-education-department-student-loans/story?id=118730549.

[53] U.S. Department of Energy, "Universities," Office of Science, accessed December 17, 2025, www.energy.gov/science/universities.

[54] U.S. Department of Education, "Statement on President Trump's Executive Order to Return Power Over Education to States and Local Communities," press release, March 20, 2025, www.ed.gov/about/news/press-release/statement-president-trumps-executive-order-return-power-over-education-states-and-local-communities;

[55] U.S. Department of Education, "U.S. Department of Education Announces Six New Agency Partnerships."

[56] White House, "White House Initiative to Promote Excellence and Innovation at Historically Black Colleges and Universities," Executive Order, April 23, 2025, www.whitehouse.gov/presidential-actions/2025/04/white-house-initiative-to-promote-excellence-and-innovation-at-historically-black-colleges-and-universities/.

[57] Lexi Lonas Cochran, "Sale of Student Loan Portfolio Could Be Next Target of Trump Education Department," *The Hill*, November 18, 2025, thehill.com/homenews/education/5609708-trump-education-department-student-loan-portfolio-sale/.

[58] Ayanna Pressley, "Pressley, Warren, Sanders, Over 40 Lawmakers Urge Trump Administration to End Plans to Sell Federal Student Loan Portfolio," press release, November 17, 2025, pressley.house.gov/2025/11/17/pressley-warren-sanders-over-40-lawmakers-urge-trump-administration-to-end-plans-to-sell-federal-student-loan-portfolio/.

[59] Jen Smith, "Trump Aims to Control NIH Research Priorities and Cut the Agency's Budget by Billions," *Cancer Therapy Advisor*, May 5, 2025, www.cancertherapyadvisor.com/features/trump-aims-to-control-nih-research-and-cut-budget/.

[60] Regina Sienra, "U.S. Government To No Longer Regard Architecture, Education, and Nursing as Professional Degrees," *My Modern Met*, December 1, 2025, mymodernmet.com/professional-degrees-loans-archictecture-education/; Jessica Blake, "What to Know About Trump's Definition of Professional Degrees," *Inside Higher Ed*, November 26, 2025, www.insidehighered.com/news/government/student-aid-policy/2025/11/26/what-know-about-definition-professional-degree.

[61] Felix Salmon, "Business CEOs can say whatever they want now," *Axios,* Jan 16, 2025, www.axios.com/2025/01/16/ceo-trump-zuckerberg-musk-thiel

[62] Exec. Order No. 14,142, 3 C.F.R. (2025), www.whitehouse.gov/presidential-actions/2025/12/eliminating-state-law-obstruction-of-national-artificial-intelligence-policy/.

[63] Ibid.

[64] "Education," AI.gov, accessed December 17, 2025, www.ai.gov/initiatives/education.

[65] Sasha Rogelberg, "The U.S. spent $30 billion to ditch textbooks for laptops and tablets," *Forbes,* February 21, 2026, https://fortune.com/2026/02/21/laptops-tablets-schools-gen-z-less-cognitively-capable-parents-first-time-cellphone-bans-standardized-test-scores/

[66] Ibid.

[67] White House, "Advancing Artificial Intelligence Education for American Youth," Executive Order, April 23, 2025, www.whitehouse.gov/presidential-actions/2025/04/advancing-artificial-intelligence-education-for-american-youth/.

[68] Ibid.

[69] Nolan Higdon, "Randi Weingarten's AI Betrayal," *Critical Media Literacy with Nolan Higdon* (Substack), August 1, 2025, nolanhigdon.substack.com/p/randi-weingartens-ai-betrayal.

[70] Gary Smith, "Illusions: No, Large Language Models Do Not Understand

A recent New Yorker article is mistaken about this," *Mind Matters,* November 14, 2025 6mindmatters.ai/2025/11/illusions-no-large-language-models-do-not-understand/

[71] Shojaee, Parshin, Iman Mirzadeh, Keivan Alizadeh, Maxwell Horton, Samy Bengio, and Mehrdad Farajtabar, "The Illusion of Thinking: Understanding the Strengths and Limitations of Reasoning Models via the Lens of Problem Complexity," Paper presented at the 39th Conference on Neural Information Processing Systems (NeurIPS), June 2025, machinelearning.apple.com/research/illusion-of-thinking.

[72] Joanna Stern, "We Let AI Run Our Office Vending Machine. It Lost Hundreds of Dollars," *Wall Street Journal,* December 18, 2025,

www.wsj.com/tech/ai/anthropic-claude-ai-vending-machine-agent-b7e84e34.

[73] Broussard, *More than a Glitch.*

[74] TOI Tech Desk, "Elon Musk's Grok in Trouble: Makes Racist Comments, Calls Itself 'MechaHitler'; Company Deletes Offensive Posts," *Times of India,* July 9, 2025, timesofindia.indiatimes.com/technology/tech-news/elon-musks-grok-in-trouble-makes-racist-comments-calls-itself-mechahitler-company-deletes-offensive-posts/articleshow/122335603.cms.

[75] Rob Kuznia, Allison Gordon, and Ed Lavandera, "'You're Not Rushing. You're Just Ready:' Parents Say ChatGPT Encouraged Son to Kill Himself," *CNN,* November 20, 2025, www.cnn.com/2025/11/06/us/openai-chatgpt-suicide-lawsuit-invs-vis; Katie McQue, "AI Is Overpowering Efforts to Catch Child Predators, Experts Warn," *The Guardian,* July 18, 2024, www.theguardian.com/technology/article/2024/jul/18/ai-generated-images-child-predators; Thorn, "AI-Generated Child Sexual Abuse: The New Digital Threat We Must Confront Now," *Thorn* (blog), August 13, 2025, www.thorn.org/blog/ai-generated-child-sexual-abuse-the-new-digital-threat-we-must-confront-now/.

[76] Josh Bersin, "BBC Finds That 45% of AI Queries Produce Erroneous Answers," *Josh Bersin* (blog), October 26, 2025 (updated October 29, 2025), joshbersin.com/2025/10/bbc-finds-that-45-of-ai-queries-produce-erroneous-answers/.

[77] Stanford Institute for Human-Centered AI, "Hallucinating Law: Legal Mistakes with Large Language Models Are Pervasive," January 11, 2024, hai.stanford.edu/news/hallucinating-law-legal-mistakes-large-language-models-are-pervasive.

[78] Max Tani, "Washington Post's AI-Generated Podcasts Rife with Errors, Fictional Quotes," *Semafor,* December 11, 2025, www.semafor.com/article/12/11/2025/washington-posts-ai-generated-podcasts-rife-with-errors-fictional-quotes.

79 Dan Mangan, "Judge Sanctions Lawyers for Brief Written by A.I. with Fake Citations," *CNBC*, June 22, 2023, www.cnbc.com/2023/06/22/judge-sanctions-lawyers-whose-ai-written-filing-contained-fake-citations.html; Jake Thomlinson, "Canadian AI Ethics Report Withdrawn Over Fabricated Citations," *ResearchWize*, November 5, 2025, www.researchwize.com/news/canadian-ai-ethics-report-withdrawn-over-fabricated-citations.

80 Michael Clune, "Colleges Are Preparing to Self-Lobotomize," *The Atlantic*, November 19, 2025, www.theatlantic.com/ideas/archive/2025/11/colleges-ai-education-students/685039/.

81 Andrew R. Chow, "ChatGPT May Be Eroding Critical Thinking Skills, According to a New MIT Study," *Time*, June 23, 2025, time.com/7295195/ai-chatgpt-google-learning-school/; Mohammed Zeinu Hassen, "The Impact of AI on Students' Reading, Critical Thinking, and Problem-Solving Skills," *American Journal of Education and Information Technology* 9, no. 2 (2025): 82–90.

82 Alex Knapp, "The Prototype: Study Suggests AI Tools Decrease Critical Thinking Skills," *Forbes*, January 10, 2025, www.forbes.com/sites/alexknapp/2025/01/10/the-prototype-study-suggests-ai-tools-decrease-critical-thinking-skills/.

83 Jennifer Vilcarino and Lauraine Langreo, "Rising Use of AI in Schools Comes With Big Downsides for Students," *Education Week*, October 8, 2025, www.edweek.org/technology/rising-use-of-ai-in-schools-comes-with-big-downsides-for-students/2025/10.

84 Ronald Purser, "AI Is Destroying the University and Learning Itself," *Current Affairs*, December 1, 2025, www.currentaffairs.org/news/ai-is-destroying-the-university-and-learning-itself.

85 Associated Press, "Penn to Ban Trans Women from Women's Sports, Ends Case Focused on Lia Thomas," *ESPN*, July 1, 2025, www.espn.com/college-sports/story/_/id/45634254/penn-ban-trans-athletes-ending-lia-thomas-civil-rights-case; Jake Offenhartz, "Columbia University Agrees to Policy Changes after Trump Administration Funding Threats," *PBS NewsHour*, March 21, 2025, www.pbs.org/newshour/education/columbia-university-agrees-to-policy-changes-after-trump-administration-funding-threats; Brown University, "Federal Agreement FAQs: Brown's Sex and Gender Policies and Gender-Affirming Care," Office of Equity Compliance and Reporting, accessed December 17, 2025, campus-life.brown.edu/oecr/faq-sex-and-gender; Sam Levin, "UC Berkeley Shares 160 Names with Trump Administration in 'McCarthy Era' Move," *The Guardian*, September 12, 2025,

www.theguardian.com/us-news/2025/sep/12/uc-berkeley-trump-administration-antisemitism.

[86] Natalie Schwartz, "'A Dangerous Precedent': Critics Slam Columbia's Agreement with Trump Administration," *Higher Ed Dive*, July 24, 2025, www.highereddive.com/news/critics-slam-trump-deal-columbia/753991/.

[87] Jackson Dilks and Alexis Hernandez Lopez, "Columbia Drops to No. 15 in U.S. News Best National Universities Ranking, Lowest of the Ivies," *Columbia Daily Spectator*, September 24, 2025, www.columbiaspectator.com/news/2025/09/24/columbia-drops-to-no-15-in-us-news-best-national-universities-ranking-lowest-of-the-ivies/.

[88] Katherine Knott, "How Universities Are Responding to Trump's Compact," *Inside Higher Ed,* October 24, 2025

www.insidehighered.com/news/government/2025/10/24/how-universities-are-responding-trumps-compact

[89] Taylor Romine and Betsy Klein, "7 Universities Reject White House Funding Deal with Attached Demands," *CNN*, October 23, 2025, www.cnn.com/2025/10/16/us/trump-universities-compact-funding.

[90] Greta Díaz González Vázquez, "UT Austin Is One of Two Universities That Hasn't Rejected Trump Administration's Funding Compact," *KUT 90.5*, October 21, 2025, www.keranews.org/education/2025-10-21/university-of-texas-austin-trump-funding-compact.

[91] Susan Jones, comp., "Higher Ed Update: UVA First Public School to Reach Deal with Administration on DEI," *University Times* (University of Pittsburgh) 58, no. 5, October 24, 2025, www.utimes.pitt.edu/news/higher-ed-update-uva.

[92] Brown University, "Brown University President Declines Invitation for Brown to Join Federal Compact," news release, October 15, 2025, www.brown.edu/news/2025-10-15/brown-response-federal-compact; WJAR Staff, "Brown University Enters Agreement with Federal Government to Restore Research Funding," *KOMO News*, July 30, 2025, komonews.com/news/nation-world/brown-university-enters-agreement-with-federal-government-to-restore-research-funding-trump-nondiscrimination-grants-compliance-july-30-2025.

[93] American Association of University Professors, "AAUP Case Challenging the Trump Administration's Executive Orders Seeking to Ban Diversity, Equity, and Inclusion Programs," accessed December 18, 2025, www.aaup.org/aaup-case-challenging-trump-administrations-executive-orders-seeking-ban-diversity-equity-and; American Association of University Professors, "Win in *AAUP v. Trump*: Court Blocks Attacks on University of California System," news release, December 18, 2025, www.aaup.org/news/win-aaup-v-trump-court-blocks-attacks-university-california-system.

94 Alice Speri, "Students and Faculty at Over 100 US Universities Protest Against Trump's Attacks," *The Guardian*, November 7, 2025, www.theguardian.com/us-news/2025/nov/07/student-protest-trump-education-attacks.

95 EdSource Staff, "Trump Administration Ordered to Restore $500 Million in Research Grants to UCLA," *EdSource*, September 23, 2025, edsource.org/updates/trump-administration-ucla-funding.

96 Jaweed Kaleem, "Times Investigation: Ex-Trump DOJ Lawyers Say 'Fraudulent' UC Antisemitism Probes Led Them to Quit," *Los Angeles Times*, December 13, 2025, www.latimes.com/california/story/2025-12-13/former-doj-attorneys-university-of-california-ucla-antisemitism-investigation; Peter Elkind and Katherine Mangan, "The Shakedown:

Trump's DOJ Pressured Lawyers to 'Find' Evidence That UCLA Had Illegally Tolerated Antisemitism," *ProPublica*, December 12, 2025, www.propublica.org/article/ucla-antisemitism-investigation-trump-doj.

97 Eric He, "No Deal, No Defiance: UC's Trump Fight Grinds On, Leaving UCLA in Limbo," *Politico*, December 28, 2025, www.politico.com/news/2025/12/28/uc-facultys-fight-with-trump-has-put-the-university-in-a-tough-spot-00694193.

98 Associated Press, "Judge Indefinitely Bars Trump from Fining UC over Alleged Discrimination," *NPR*, November 15, 2025, www.npr.org/2025/11/15/nx-s1-5609876/uc-university-california-discrimination-fine-ruling.

99 EdSource Staff, "Trump Administration Drops Appeal of $1.2 Billion Fine Against UCLA," *EdSource*, February 20, 2026, edsource.org/updates/trump-administration-drops-appeal-of-1-2-billion-fine-against-ucla.

Chapter 6

1 Ariana Baio, "As Trump Works to Build His $400M Ballroom at the White House, Officials Say No More Construction Projects Are Planned," *The Independent*, December 24, 2025, www.the-independent.com/news/world/americas/us-politics/white-house-ballroom-construction-b2890283.html.

2 Luke Broadwater, "Inside Trump's Push to Make the White House Ballroom as Big as Possible," *New York Times*, November 29, 2025, www.nytimes.com/2025/11/29/us/politics/trump-white-house-ballroom.html.

3 Bernd Debusmann Jr., "Who Is Paying for Trump's White House Ballroom? Full Donor List Revealed," *BBC News*, October 23, 2025, www.bbc.com/news/articles/c891yxgj44ko.

4 Economist Intelligence Unit, *Democracy Index 2024*, London: EIU, 2024,

www.eiu.com/n/campaigns/democracy-index-2024.

[5] Jesse Colombo, "America's Wealth Inequality Is At Roaring Twenties Levels," *Forbes*, February 28, 2019, www.forbes.com/sites/jessecolombo/2019/02/28/americas-wealth-inequality-is-at-roaring-twenties-levels/; U.S. Department of Health and Human Services, *Poverty in the United States: 50-Year Trends and Safety Net Impacts*, March 2016, aspe.hhs.gov/sites/default/files/migrated_legacy_files/142581/50YearTrends.pdf; Urban Institute, "Nine Charts about Wealth Inequality in America," April 25, 2024, apps.urban.org/features/wealth-inequality-charts/.

[6] Aaron McDade, "Here's How Many Americans Can't Afford a $400 Emergency—The Numbers May Shock You," *Investopedia*, September 22, 2025, www.investopedia.com/here-s-how-many-americans-can-t-afford-a-usd400-emergency-the-numbers-may-shock-you-11814788; Institute on Taxation and Economic Policy, "Child Poverty Remains Unacceptably High, New Federal Changes Unlikely to Move Needle," September 16, 2025, itep.org/child-poverty-remains-unacceptably-child-tax-credit-changes/; Annie E. Casey Foundation, "Measuring Access to Opportunity in the United States: A 10-Year Update," October 20, 2025, www.aecf.org/resources/measuring-access-to-opportunity-in-the-united-states-a-10-year-update.

[7] Pixelsand8, "Yes, I Am Blaming Neoliberalism for the Florida School Shooting," *Writers Without Money*, February 15, 2018, writerswithoutmoney.com/2018/02/15/yes-i-am-blaming-neoliberalism-for-the-florida-school-shootings/; Kevin Sapere, "'Going Postal': Neoliberalism and Mass Shootings," *Left Voice*, August 12, 2019, www.leftvoice.org/going-postal-neoliberalism-and-mass-shootings/; Anoop Mirpuri, "Racial Violence, Mass Shootings, and the U.S. Neoliberal State," *Critical Ethnic Studies* 2, no. 1 (Spring 2016): 73–106

[8] Rita Mae Brown, *Sudden Death: A Novel* (New York: Bantam Books, 1984).

[9] Jaweed Kaleem and Jocelyn Gecker, "AI Is Scoring College Essays and Conducting Interviews, a New Layer in Admissions Stress," *Los Angeles Times*, January 2, 2026, www.latimes.com/california/story/2026-01-02/ai-may-be-scoring-your-college-admissions-essay.

[10] Nataliya Kosmyna, Eugene Hauptmann, Ye Tong Yuan, Jessica Situ, Xian-Hao Liao, Ashly Vivian Beresnitzky, Iris Braunstein, and Pattie Maes, "Your Brain on ChatGPT: Accumulation of Cognitive Debt when Using an AI Assistant for Essay Writing Task," arXiv preprint, submitted June 13, 2025, arxiv.org/pdf/2506.08872v1.

[11] Nolan Higdon, "The Price of Comfort: How Corporate Media Left Democrats Blindsided in 2024 (Again)," *The Edge*, November 13, 2024,

www.theedgemedia.org/price-comfort-how-corporate-media-left-democrats-blindsided-2024-again/; Carter Sherman, "2024 US Elections Takeaways: How Female Voters Broke for Harris and Trump," *The Guardian*, November 6, 2024, www.theguardian.com/us-news/2024/nov/06/election-trump-harris-women-voters.

[12] ABC News, "Hillary Clinton Officially Wins Popular Vote by Nearly 2.9 Million," December 22, 2016, abcnews.go.com/Politics/hillary-clinton-officially-wins-popular-vote-29-million/story?id=44354341.

[13] Peter Suciu, "Social Media 'Sympathy' For Luigi Mangione Risks Jury Nullification," *Forbes*, December 16, 2024, www.forbes.com/sites/petersuciu/2024/12/16/social-media-sympathy-for-luigi-mangione-risks-jury-nullification/.

[14] Goddard, et al., *The Civic University*; Goddard, *Learning for Work*.

[15] Putnam, *Bowling Alone*.

[16] John Saltmarsh, "Education for Critical Citizenship: John Dewey's Contribution to the Pedagogy of Community," *Michigan Journal of Community Service Learning* 3 (1996): 13–21.

[17] Nick Hanauer, "The Top 1% of Americans Have Taken $50 Trillion From the Bottom 90%—And That's Made the U.S. Less Secure," *Time*, September 14, 2020, time.com/5888024/50-trillion-income-inequality-america/.

[18] Ben Casselman and Colby Smith, "Wealthy Americans Are Spending. People With Less Are Struggling," *New York Times*, October 19, 2025, www.nytimes.com/2025/10/19/business/economic-divide-spending-inflation-jobs.html.

[19] Nolan Higdon, "Decoding Epstein: A Healthy Skeptic's Guide to the Epstein Saga," February 2026, nolanhigdon.substack.com/p/decoding-epstein

[20] Phillip Levine, "Should College Endowments Be Taxed?" *Brookings*, September 3, 2024, www.brookings.edu/articles/should-college-endowments-be-taxed/.

[21] Bloomberg, "Wealthiest Colleges Fight to Protect Endowments from Taxation," *Pensions & Investments*, March 10, 2025, www.pionline.com/endowments-and-foundations/wealthiest-colleges-fight-protect-endowments-taxation/.

www.ingramcontent.com/pod-product-compliance
Lightning Source LLC
Chambersburg PA
CBHW041158150726
48006CB00016B/2032